MARRIAGE AND FAMILY LIFE

A CHRISTIAN PERSPECTIVE

BY STAN E. DEKOVEN PH.D.

Stan E. DeKoven Ph.D.

MARRIAGE AND FAMILY LIFE

A CHRISTAN PERSPECTIVE

COPYRIGHT © 1994 STAN E. DEKOVEN

SECOND EDITION, 2007

BY STAN E. DEKOVEN, PH.D.

ISBN: 1-931178-17-8

FOR ORDERING INFORMATION, PLEASE CONATCT:

VISION PUBLISHING
1115 D STREET, RAMONA CALIFORNIA
www.visionpublishingservices.com
1-800-9-VISION

DEDICATION

First of all, this book is dedicated to the many loving parents who have been role models of love and affirmation, beginning with my very own Mom and Dad. In addition, I would like to dedicate this book to the many families that I have had the privilege of ministering to in the course of my work and training as a Pastor, Educator and a Marriage and Family Therapist.

Finally, I would dedicate this book to the vast family of God, to whom I have had the privilege of being sent in years past. The Family of God and the families of mankind are both miraculous and awesome to behold. Let me close my dedication with this final thought from the heart of the Father.

> *"Blessed be the God and Father of our Lord Jesus Christ, who hath blessed us with all spiritual blessings in heavenly places in Christ. According as he hath chosen us in him before the foundation of the world, that we should be holy without blame before him, in love. Having predestinated us unto the adoption of sons by Jesus Christ to himself, according to the good pleasure of His will. To the praise of the glory of his grace, through which he hath made us accepted in the Beloved."*
> Ephesians 1:3-6

AUTHOR'S FORWARD

Many times our studies will help increase our intellectual knowledge, but they do not always impact our individual need to grow into maturity and become the total human beings that God intended us to be.

This book is specifically designed to encourage and help the reader to fully engage in the task of learning and growing in the knowledge of the development process of Christian families.

A fundamental premise of this book is that the best kind of learning occurs when the student is actively involved in the process of learning.

The best education consists not of simply knowing, but of becoming; that is, becoming all that God created us to be.

The format of this book briefly examines the external structures of family life throughout the cycle of human existence, from a Christian perspective. It also teaches the student how to communicate and interact in more conscious, deliberate and constructive ways. He or she can then become more fulfilled in his or her intimate relationships. The natural family and the family of God are the most dynamic institutions formed by God. They are worthy of deeper understanding. My hope is that both understanding and the wisdom to apply what is learned, will be a natural outgrowth of this work.

STAN E. DEKOVEN PH.D.

PREFACE

BY: DR. JASON GUERRERO

"You cannot teach, what you do not know!"
"You cannot reap, where you did not sow!"
"You cannot lead, where you will not go!
                                        -Unknown-

For me to say that families are very important to God would be quite an understatement, but in today's fast paced and rapidly changing social currents the health of both *"Marriage"* and *"Family"* is coming under ever increasing amounts of pressure. The term *"Family Values"* is being thrown around rather loosely in today's popular culture and the societal definition of that term varies from one group of individuals to another. Discussions of what is a "real family" versus what isn't have caused many people's personal views to become blurred and twisted, as to what their own personal responsibilities are or should be within the family.

God knows everything there is to know about families because He created them! He indeed, knows how to make both marriages and families function to their greatest and highest potential. Since He alone is the only truly original "Father," He has a vested interest in seeing that every one of His family fully understands the greatness of His plan for "The Family." God's answers to this generation's difficulties the arenas of "Marriage and the Family" are the answers we can count on to produce the love, intimacy and joy that were His original intent when He initialized the very first family

In Dr. DeKoven's book on Marriage and Family Life, God's answers to mankind's "family problems" are related in detail. From foundational issues to practical applications, the pastor, student, and professional counselor will find substantive, scriptural and Spirit anointed direction for those in need. For those in difficulty; solutions will be made clearer than ever before. For those already in successful marriages and good families; growth, insight and enrichment of intimacy will improve that which is already good. For those who counsel and comfort the wounded; sensitivity, insight and personal empathy will enable them to better affect healing in the lives of the broken. It is my prayer that God will use this text to maximize both "your family" and "His Family."

II Corinthians 1:3-4,

> *"Blessed be God, even the Father of our Lord Jesus Christ, the Father of all mercies, and the God of all comfort, Who comforteth us in all our tribulations, that we may be able to comfort them who are in any trouble, with the same comfort with which we ourselves are comforted by God."*

TABLE OF CONTENTS

INTRODUCTION
(THE SECOND EDITION)

Since the writing of the first edition of this work, much has happened in the world. In the West, we have bee rocked by 9/11 and the war on terrorism, and the cultural wars have kicked into high gear (the push towards same sex marriage, etc.). Many outstanding ministries are attempting to address the issues that affect our families and erode our Christian values. Pastors and other spiritual leaders, recognizing the importance of family life are teaching on an annual basis principles of family life. All of the efforts being made are encouraging, yet the trends in the Western culture continue towards degeneration of marriage and family life as seen in a continued high divorce rate, abuse in the family and out of control children running the home. Much finger pointing and hand wringing could ensure from what we see, but Christian's have not been called to criticize but to conquer, as we live out the principles of God's word in the families, churches and communities in which we live.

It is true, problems continue, and the war on terror against the family seems difficult at best. Yet, as we read God's word we are continuously reminded that where sin abounds, grace does much more abound. In fact, it takes abounding grace to minister to, live in and hope for healthy families.

Another observation that has become a painful reality to most is the fact that no marriage is made in heaven; even the best of God's people can fail, and no family is, was or will be perfect. This cruel myth of perfection, perpetuated by many teachers, even well intended ones, is not remotely rooted in truth. Happily ever after is a fairytale, but joyful, loving, fulfilling even fun can and should be our experience in a Christian home, as we apply the principles of God's word to our lives.

I am reminded of a family who started life with the best of intentions. George and Sharon[1] had been married for 7 years when I met them. They were referred for counseling by their pastor. The pastor had spent good quality care with them in prayer and bible study, but soon realized that their problems seemed a bit beyond his expertise and allowable time.

When I first met this couple they appeared to be a delightful pair. He was a software engineer making better than average income, she worked part time for another church as an administrative assistant. They had two children, ages 4 and 2, a little by and girl.

Both stated their commitment to Christ and to marriage and family. Both shared passionately how much they wanted their marriage to work. Both were extremely unhappy, burdened by financial stress, lack of love (her view) and respect (his). Both wondered if their present existence was all there was for them. After assuring them (in faith) that certainly their lives could be better, we began to explore over several weeks their story.

Not uncommonly, they had entered the marriage with many expectations of what needs were to be met in marriage. Many of these assumptions were not based on reality. Further, they were beginning to manifest patterns from their parents marriages (quite unconsciously) that

---

[1] The story is true, but the names and situations have been rearranged to insure anonymity.

frankly, scared them when finally revealed. Finally, they had developed their own dysfunctional patterns of communication, effecting attitudes towards each other and their intimate life.

Over a period of several months, these honest strugglers were able to, by God's grace, learn and apply some basic principles of common sense and the world of God, which over time brought heir family ship into safer waters. Much of their problems with each other were rooted in hurts and misunderstandings, but most were a result of generational patterns learned in the family of origin and assumed to be "normal and correct". Their lack of knowledge, understanding and wisdom found in the word of God, lead to their difficulties.

Well, George and Sharon made adjustments and are living out a reasonably well adjusted and fulfilling marriage. The same is possible for any sincere man and woman who in like manner are willing to appropriate principles of truth from God's word and good sense to their lives.

Stan E. DeKoven Ph.D.

INTRODUCTION
THE BROKEN CIRCLE

I was twenty-one years old when my beautiful bride and I took that long walk down the aisle of the church. We were both so very excited to finally make official what we were completely sure of. We were made for each other, forever! I still remember with great fondness when I look back at that marvelous event.

One of the most touching parts of our ceremony was the exchanging of our rings. The minister recited to us the symbolic significance of this act. The ring symbolized our never ending love and devotion to each other. The circle of love which was never to be broken. Never!

Well, that's the way it was meant to be. Though we had our fair share of crisis times in our marriage and family, we happily survived. Yet, this is not so for many friends and family members. Though many Christian couples state the same vows as we did, for all to many, the eternally pledged circle is broken. But why?

In The United States today approximately 50% of marriages end in divorce, (Evangelical Christian marriages are not significantly better), thousands of children are abused physically and sexually, wives are battered, children run away, over 6,000 adolescents annually commit suicide, and families disintegrate. The pressures of our world are immense and most difficult to cope with. Even in our churches we are confronted with the "besetting sins" (Heb. 12:1) that destroy the circle that was to be unbroken.

Over the past few years, it has been my privilege to work

with many families who were at their breaking point. There has been a renewed interest amongst the secular and Christian circles alike to at least recognize and acknowledge the immensity of the family breakdown. As impressive as the statistics of divorce, abuse and self-destruction may be, there remain mixed views amongst the church of Jesus Christ as to how we should approach the wounded or broken family. It is apparent that something must be done to stem the tide. This book is one persons attempt to help marriages start out right and for families to move forward in patterns of health.

STRUCTURE OF THIS BOOK

This book has been developed for easy application. To ensure a progressive flow, it is organized on the principle of first things first. That is, the reader should begin as God did, with the creation of man, the expression of His purposes, and the foundation of relationships - marriage. This comprises Section I of this book.

Section II focuses directly on family life, especially parenting, beginning when the first child emerges on the scene. Family life in the western world has become increasingly complex, rife with potential pitfalls. These will be discussed in light of scriptural principles. Every family is uniquely constituted. Thus, the challenges that each family faces is equally unique.

In Section III special concerns that may be faced in family life are developed. This is followed with a bibliography and glossary of terms that will prove valuable for furthermore research and information.

The final section is written with some trepidation. I will attempt to present some fairly complex information on counseling troubled families in a simplified form. Essentially, my hope is to provide the Christian and professional with a counseling model to assist in the understanding, diagnosis and treating of the symptoms of marital and family dysfunction at a beginning professional level. This is by no means a comprehensive approach, but a broad strokes application of therapeutic techniques and models that have been helpful in my counseling ministry. It is not a substitute for advanced clinical training.

MY PURPOSE

This book is written as a teaching/training tool for pastors, counselors and church leaders who desire to be a part of stemming the tide of family dysfunction and providing a firm foundation for marriage and family life. It is the authors' assumption that a major function of the church is to rebuild the walls of people's lives and to repair the breaches or broken places. (Isa. 58:12)

To repair or restore the broken places takes knowledge and wisdom. The knowledge required is acquired by thoroughly understanding the intent of the original builder. Since God is the author of the family, and His word is the manual containing the foundational plan, we must seek His plan and purpose first. Wisdom speaks of the application of God's principles to the exact areas of need, with grace, mercy and love.

Every man and woman called to marriage and family life have a supreme desire to be successful in this life long endeavor. The circle of life is to be unbroken, and to ensure greater success there must be a thorough understanding of God's plan.

SECTION I

MARRIAGE

FOUNDATION OF THE FAMILY OF GOD

"It takes two to make marriage a success and only one a failure."

Herbert Samuel

Stan E. DeKoven Ph.D.

SECTION I

INTRODUCTION TO THE FAMILY CRUCIBLE

Carl A. Whitaker, M.D. and Augustas Y. Napier, Ph.D. wrote an excellent book on troubled families called "THE FAMILY CRUCIBLE." They very ably describe the many forces, interpsychic and societal, that tear away at the very fabric of the family. Today, we see thousands of Christian families, members of the Body of Christ that is His Church, torn apart by forces which are often misunderstood. The Church has a tremendous opportunity to assist the troubled family and strengthen the Body of Christ if we can learn to recognize the causes and potential cures for family distress.

To ignore the extensive nature of this problem should be as anathema as it is to ignore that "all have sinned." It is my hope that all Christians might be fully equipped to minister to those who are in a time of intense need, to those who are in the family crucible.

> Scripture: Matt. 25:34-40, New American
> Standard
> "Then shall the King say unto them on his right hand, Come, ye blessed of my Father, inherit the kingdom prepared for you from the foundation of the world: For I was a hungered, and ye gave me meat: I was thirsty, and ye gave me drink; I was a stranger, and ye took me in: Naked, and ye clothes me: I was sick, and ye visited me: I was in prison, and ye came unto me. Then shall the righteous answer him, saying, Lord, when saw we thee a hungered, and fed thee? or thirsty, and gave thee drink? When saw we thee a stranger,

and took thee in? or naked, and clothed thee? Or when saw we thee sick, or in prison, and came unto thee? And the King shall answer and say unto them, Verily I say unto you, Inasmuch as ye have done it unto one of the least of these my brethren, ye have done it unto me."

The purpose of this section is to educate, inform, and hopefully strengthen the Christian family by presenting basic marriage and family life principles from a Biblical perspective. It is the premise of this book that the judicious application of Biblical principles on marriage and family life will bring honor to the Lord, strengthen family life, and increase the quality of life for each individual. The enemy of our souls has for too long had the upper hand in undermining the fabric of family life. It's time the church and the people of God begin to erase that trend. For we *"can do all things through Christ who strengthens me."* Phil. 4:13.

DEFINITION OF MARRIAGE

Our society continues to attempt to define marriage in ways contrary to the Biblical record: marriage is an institution ordained by God. Basically, the Christian view of marriage is not that it is primarily or essentially a binding legal and social contract. The Christian understands marriage as a covenant made before God and in the presence of fellow members of the Christian family. Such a pledge endures, not because of the force of law or the fear of its sanctions, but because an unconditional covenant has been made. A covenant more solemn, more binding, more permanent than any legal contract.

It can be furthermore defined as "a system by means of which persons who are sinful and contentious are so caught up by a dream and a purpose bigger than themselves that they work through the years, in spite of repeated disappointment, to make the dream come true."[2]

Marriage is a relationship between man and woman intended by God to be a monogamous joining, intended to be a permanent bond in which many needs are satisfied - the need to love and be loved, the need for deep friendship, for sharing, for companionship, for sexual satisfaction, for children, the need to escape loneliness. Marriage ought to be a bond of love, reflecting the love Christ has for His people, a bond of sacrificial love where husband and wife have become one.

You may have a slightly different interpretation of what marriage is all about. In reality most of us come into the marital relationship with certain specific beliefs and expectations in regards to what marriage is. As frightening as this may sound, most of us learn about marriage by living in our family of origin. It is there that we have observed our mother's and father's marriage relationship. Whether we admit it or not, we carry within our minds (at a sub or unconscious level) a definition of marriage, a belief system of what marriage is about, with subsequent roles and expectations that we think our partner and we ourselves should fulfill. All of these make marriage a potentially exciting and wonderful experience, yet potentially detrimental and destructive.

From the definition (conscious or not, we have inherited or developed, a philosophy of marriage and family emerges.

---

[2] Author of quote unknown.

This foundational belief is rarely challenged prior to saying, "I do." Thus, most couples enter marriage with a romanticized view that is all too quickly destroyed by life's realities. Unless our basic beliefs and philosophy have been successfully modified by God's word and practical realities, we are destined to repeat certain ingrained patterns that we are convinced are "truth." In rebuilding (or building) a solid Christian foundation of marriage and family life, we must begin by understanding a Biblical philosophy of marriage and goals for marriage and family life.

BIBLICAL GOALS FOR MARRIAGE

PROBLEMS STATED

Marriage is the foundation of family life. A healthy, strong foundation is essential for a family to grow.

Our generation is characterized by many conflicting philosophies and value systems. Some advocate a variety of marriage forms (e.g. contractual, communal, "living together," etc.) easy divorces, and experimental sexual relationships. There is overwhelming evidence that such life styles produce tragic results: growing numbers of disillusioned persons and many deprived, disturbed children, not to mention the growing tragedy of AIDS. What is to be the church's response? What should it be? Only the leading of God's Word and Spirit can provide the needed perspective. Each Biblical concept offers positive guidance and combats numerous misconceptions. When taught with sensitivity by elders, pastors, teachers, and parents, God's special design for married life and human sexuality can prevent painful lives and offer therapeutic help to the wounded. The Word of God calls us to repentance and deep maturity in matters such as these.

The Biblical understanding of marriage is related to the nature and purpose of God. Biblical views of man, marriage, sex, and family refuse to explain life in terms of man's self-chosen aims. The Bible insists that attempts to understand life apart from the divine purpose are ultimately foolish. The Creator's design establishes the dignity of the divine gift of marriage. Within the Word we find three primary goals for marriage and Family life.

MARRIAGE IS FOR FELLOWSHIP

Men and women were created for fellowship with God and for His glory. Their dignity rests in their relational capacity. Men and women were designed for fellowship with each other and for fellowship in the greater human community (Gen. 2; Ex. 20:2-17; Isa. 11:6ff; 54:1-3; Matt. 19:4-11; Jn. 15:1-17; 17:6-26; Eph. 1:9-10, 2:13-21). Marriage and human sexuality cannot be understood simply as the result of physical drives, rational formulations, social imposition, or religious moralism. While marital union is not in the realm of things commanded by God (as are fellowship with God and his people), it is a divine gift not to be profaned. The intimacy of marriage gives expression to the human desire for relatedness. The relationship of husband and wife is often compared to the reciprocal relationship of God and his people and is described in the language of the covenant. The covenant between God and his people is sacred and is not to be violated. It has great power and purpose in it. (Isa. 61:10; Hosea; Jn. 3:29; Eph. 2:19-22). Marriage is a covenant bond designed by the Creator, it is redeemed in Jesus Christ, and is best realized amidst the Covenant people of God.

MARRIAGE IS FOR HUMAN FULFILLMENT

Marriage is designed to bring persons into their God-intended human fullness. Humanity in it's wholeness involves both male and female. The interdependence so essential to human completeness can be expressed in marital union and also in the larger community. In marital union, husband and wife become "one flesh" (Gen. 2:24).[3] This unity involves far more than a sexual encounter, it is the joining of lives at many levels. With it come mutual love and knowledge. Marriage provides opportunity for mature love so vital to the wholeness of persons (Gen. 24:67; Prov. 5:15-19; Song of Sol. 1; 2:16, 8:7; Eph. 5:21-33.). Marriage is a covenant commitment which protects the mutuality of sex and the meaning of personhood. It acknowledges responsibility for the continued well-being of another person. God is concerned about marriage because he is concerned for people. (Mal. 2:13-16). Christ heals those broken by marital and sexual sins that they might again become whole persons.

MARRIAGE IS FOR FAMILY

No better means has been devised for the rearing of each new generation and for the nurture of persons than the family. Concern for the family is found in the Old Testament (Deut. 6:7, 20ff; Hosea; Proverbs; etc.), in Jesus' ministry (Matt. 19:13-15), and in the life of the early church (Acts 2:39; 16:15; 31-33; 18:8, I Cor. 1:16; 7:12-14). Much of the responsibility for a child's instruction and for incorporation of the child into the covenant community rests with the parents. Husband and wife are often the

---

[3] One flesh does not mean the obliteration or blending of two personalities, thus eliminating individuality. Oneness denotes completeness, not sameness.

means for each other's consecration (I Cor. 7:14). In covenant relationships, marriage and family are regularly linked with God's saving and preserving work.

Several months ago I had the privilege of working with a young family that was having difficulties in their marital relationship. Both of them came into their marriage with great expectations and hope for a relationship that would fulfill all of the basic needs described above. Yet in spite of their sincere effort, they were failing miserably in their attempt to create a marriage that was fulfilling for both of them. During the course of our working together, we found that one of the many difficult issues that they had not faced was one of definition, "what is the basis for our marital union?" They had yet to determine corollary questions such as what was their marriage all about. What did covenant really mean? It was apparent with this couple, as with many, that understanding the basic principals of God's Word as they relate to how a marriage is supposed to be was essential to their healing and restoration. God has much to say in his Word about family life. Knowledge of the principles of God's word judiciously applied with love and wisdom will help to develop a healthy marriage and family.

Let us first review the Old Testament concepts for marriage and family life.

AN OLD TESTAMENT VIEW OF MARRIAGE AND THE FAMILY

IN THE BEGINNING

Within the Old Testament provides a very specific view of the way men and women are supposed to be and the basic principles for family life. One key principle of hermeneutics is based upon the premises that if you want to find God's intention for something, find the place of its first mention. When it comes to marriage and family life, we start in Genesis, Chapters 1- 3, were God's plan and pattern begins with God's original design,

> Gen. 1:26-28 says, NAS
> *"And God said, Let us make man in our own image, after our likeness; and let them have dominion over the fish of the sea, and over the fowl of the air, and over the cattle, and over all the earth, and over every creeping thing that creepeth upon the earth. So God created man in his own image, in the image of God created he him; male and female created he them. And God blessed them, and God said unto them, Be fruitful, and multiply, and fill the earth, and subdue it; and have dominion over the fish of the sea, and over the fowl of the air, and over every living thing that moveth upon the earth."*

When man or mankind was created by God, they were created perfect and complete in all aspects, spirit, soul and body. In this passage there are three Hebrew words which relate God's purpose for man, male and female.

The first is the word *Tselem* (image), which is translated shade, illusion, resemblance or representative figure. It speaks of the imprint of God on man resident in man's spirit. Prior to sin, the spirit of man was in perfect communion with God (who is spirit). Contained in the spirit of man is a representative figure or resemblance of God Himself.

Secondly, we see the word *Demwuth*, which comes from a root word *Damah* (likeness), which means resemblance, model shape or fashion and speaks of the soul or personality/character of man. This character or personality was without distortion, was untwisted by sin or the sin nature, and thus would have carried the very thoughts and beliefs of God (the mind of Christ). From this character (fruit of the Spirit), would flow the purpose of mankind, again both male and female.

The third word, *Rudah*, is translated dominion, to subjugate, prevail, reign or subdue. The purpose for mankind was to have dominion or to rule as the representative or ambassador of God over all that He had created. Of course, prior to the fall, they would have done so in perfect harmony with the nature of God, flowing from the spirit of God though the spirit of man, expressed through an unflawed soul.

In all of this wonder of creation, God's plan was always for male and female to work side by side as emissaries of the Lord here on earth. Let's take another look at how God's plan was to be expressed.

In Gen. 2:18-25, we see another important picture of God's divine plan for mankind.

> *"And the Lord God said, It is not good that the man should be alone; I will make him an help fit for him. And out of the ground the Lord God formed every beast of the field, and every fowl of the air; and brought them unto Adam to see what he would call them: and whatsoever Adam called every living creature, that was the name thereof.*

*And Adam gave names to all cattle, and to the
fowl of the air, and to every beast of the field; but
for Adam there was not found an help fit for him.
And the Lord God caused a deep sleep to fall upon
Adam, and he slept: and he took one of his ribs,
and closed up the flesh instead thereof; and the
rib, which the Lord God had taken from man,
made he a woman, and brought her unto the man.
And Adam said, This is now bone of my bones,
and flesh of my flesh; she shall be called Woman.
Therefore shall a man leave his father and
mother, and shall cleave unto his wife; and they
shall be one flesh. And they were both naked, the
man and his wife, and were not ashamed."* NAS

It should be noted that it is God Himself who recognizes
the incompleteness of man and the need for a suitable life
partner. Little needs to be said about how God created the
woman, just to note the special care the Lord took. Instead,
the focus should be on the mans' response to God's
provision, and the subsequent teaching regarding marriage
and its splendor (as ordained by God).

In vs. 23 the man awakes from his induced rest (how
wonderful that must have been) and beholds the creation of
God. She looks similar to him, yet uniquely different. He
sees her, recognizing that the answer to his heart's longing
(again, clearly recognized by the Lord) stands before him.
He states, we are the same essence, bone of bone, flesh of
flesh, and then proclaims the wondrous revelation: she is
woman. I have always sensed he proclaimed it a bit
differently, more like "wow!, man!, what a woman." "Thank
you God! I am a happy man!"

Of course, the word goes on to state a foundational truth, for this cause, a man shall leave, cleave, and become one flesh. This speaks about so much more than just the blessing of sexual intercourse, but includes a blending of two lives based upon a life long commitment of growing into a mutually beneficial covenant. The word cleave is one of the strongest words in Hebrew for joining two things together in such a way that they are inseparably bonded. The two become one, (that is complimentary, to complete each other, not sameness), setting the stage for the fulfillment of God's purpose (Gen. 2:24). Once a man and woman leave their family of origin and cleave, that bond is never to be broken. From that bond came God's command to multiply and replenish the earth.

Because there was no sin as a barrier between God and man or man and woman, they were naked, open, vulnerable and without fear or need to cover themselves, and they had no shame. Unfortunately the reality of sin impedes the development of this mystical union, and always will.

A WOMAN'S PLACE

The position of women in the marriage relationship is unique and wonderful. First of all, we must remember that God's analysis of man's situation without the woman was that it was not good. Man was by nature lonely and lacked fulfillment. Man needed a helpmate and God graciously created woman for that purpose. Woman provides a "one-flesh" relationship to man which is deeper and more important than parental ties. One of the greatest difficulties in marriage occurs when one of the partners has not been able to leave the family of origin so that they can cleave to their spouse and become "one-flesh." The deeper "one-flesh" relationship between a man and a woman is to be more important than even the early parental relationship. God initiated the marriage relationship and pronounced it to be "very good." Thus, when God sees a husband and wife living in right relationship with one another, he is well pleased. Well, this has always been God's plan for couples. As a simple observation roars, wedded life is just no that simple. The cause?...the Fall. Genesis 3:1-21 says,

> *"Now the serpent was more subtle than any beast of the field which the Lord God had made. And he said unto the woman, Yea, hath God said, Ye shall not eat of every tree of the garden? And the woman said unto the serpent, We may eat of the fruit of the trees of the garden; But of the fruit of the tree which is in the midst of the garden, God hath said, Ye shall not eat of it, neither shall ye touch it, lest ye die. And the serpent said unto the woman, Ye shall not surely die; For God doth know that in the day ye eat thereof, then your eyes shall be opened, and ye shall be as God, knowing good and evil. And when the woman saw that the tree was good for food, and that it was pleasant to the eyes, and a tree to be desired to make one wise, she took of the fruit thereof, and did eat, and gave also unto her husband with her; and he did eat. And the eyes of them both were opened, and they knew that they were naked; and they sewed fig leaves together, and made themselves aprons. And they heard the voice of the Lord God walking in the garden in the cool of the day: and Adam and his wife hid themselves from the presence of the*

*Lord God among the trees of the garden. And the
Lord God called unto Adam, and said unto him,
Where art thou? And he said, I heard thy voice in
the garden, and I was afraid, because I was
naked; and I hid myself. And he said, Who told
thee that thou wast naked? Hast thou eaten of the
tree, whereof I commanded thee that thou
shouldest not eat? And the man said, The woman
whom thou gavest to me, she gave me of the tree,
and I did eat. And the Lord God said unto the
woman, What is this that thou hast done? And the
woman said, The serpent beguiled me, and I did
eat. And the Lord God said unto the serpent,
Because thou hast done this, thou art cursed above
all cattle, and above every beast of the field; upon
thy belly shalt thou go, and dust shalt thou eat all
the days of thy life. And I will put enmity between
thee and the woman, and between thy seed and
her seed; he shall bruise thy head, and thou shalt
bruise his heel. Unto the woman he said, I will
greatly multiply thy sorrow and thy conception; in
sorrow thou shalt bring forth children; and thy
desire shall be to thy husband, and he shall rule
over thee. And unto Adam he said, Because thou
hast hearkened unto the voice of thy wife, and hast
eaten of the tree, of which I commanded thee,
saying, Thou shalt not eat of it: cursed is the
ground for thy sake; in sorrow shalt thou eat of it
all the days of thy life; Thorns also and thistles
shall it bring forth to thee; and thou shalt eat the
herb of the field; In the sweat of thy face shalt thou
eat bread, till thou return unto the ground; for out
of it wast thou taken: for dust thou art, and unto
dust shalt thou return. And Adam called his wife's*

name Eve, because she was the mother of all living. For Adam also and for his wife did the Lord God make coats of skins, and clothed them." NAS

Many important changes occurred because of Man's rebellion. In Genesis 3 we read of the fall of man from the blissful state described in chapter two. The woman is deceived by the half-truth of the serpent, eating of the forbidden fruit, and the man chooses to follow suit to both their and our destruction. Rather than focus on the act of sin itself, it is the results which are of most importance.

First, in verse 8 we observe that God is, as was the apparent pattern, searching for intimate fellowship with man (male and female) in the cool of the day. Certainly, they were well aware of God's practice, and they endeavored to hide themselves. This activity had never been necessary previously. When confronted by the voice (presence of God) of God, and finally discovered, the man proclaims his sorry state. "I heard you, I covered, I was afraid." Anxiety entered into the heart of mankind leading to defensive posturing against the voice of God. Separation by choice occurred, and has been visited to all mankind in proceeding generations.

Secondly, we see the result of sin in the relationship between the man and woman. When confronted, the man points an accusatory finger at God himself, and blames Him and the woman for his willful disobedience. My, my, how some things never change. The projection of blame, a usual response when betrayal or personal failure occurs, had begun. The woman follows his lead, placing the blame (partially justified) on the serpent.

THE BIG SHIFT

Perhaps the most devastating change that sin caused in the life of the first couple was a change of values and priorities. Prior to their rebellion, the priorities of the woman were:

- God first
- Husband Second
- Children/vocation, etc., to follow as God allowed.

In the Fall, the values/priorities shifted for the woman and all womankind to:

- Care for heath and home
- Control of the home (desire for the husband's position)
- God, of some other similar combination. The priorities of life shifted from God's intended purpose (dominion over all He created, together with her husband) to a battle for control in the home.

Of course, the man was also negatively affected. His Kingdom priorities prior to sin were:

- God First
- Wife Second
- Children/vocation, etc., to follow as God allowed.

In the Fall, the values/priorities shifted for the man, rooted in a distorted identity, from God, Spouse and Work, to;

- Work
- Work
- Work...and I do it all for you honey!

Sadly, even in the church we have virtually institutionalized these stereotypical roles as the way God intended life to be. As we will see later, this was never God's Kingdom intention, and proper values/priorities have been restored (at least potentially) through Christ finished work on the Cross.

A CLEAR PERSPECTIVE

The nature of marriage, as God designed it, is important for us to consider. The nature of marriage is a union performed by God forming one flesh of two (Gen. 2:24). Furthermore, it was initiated by God before man's fall into sin, showing it was God's original and main design, which is His best plan (Gen. 1 & 2). The idea of alternative relationships such as homosexual liaisons as being "natural" is historically and theologically ludicrous. It was never a part of God's original design for mankind. Marriage included sexuality as a normal, natural part of the relationship (Gen. 1:28 & 2:25). Again, marriage is designed and blessed (favored) by God.

The position of man in the marriage relationship was specifically stated in the book of Genesis. God gave man the responsibility of headship over the woman. Headship (properly defined as life giver or originator) meant that he was to be the primary protector and provider for his family.

Further, the man is commanded to work for his food, to provide specifically for the needs of his family. This was clearly instructed by God; a man, to be a man of God, must fulfill his responsibilities in this area. Of course, in this modern day, greater expectations have been placed upon than man than ever before. It is not enough that they be just a provider and protector, but they also need to learn to communicate effectively, with sensitivity and care, their wives. They need to love their children, while nurturing and training them. We will look more at the biblical responsibilities, through both Old and New Testament examples as we continue in this text.

God decided that marriage was pleasing to him and most excellent! One way for certain to please Him is by having a relationship with our spouse that is Biblically based (Gen. 1:31). The sanctity of intercourse in a marriage relationship is without compromise. First of all, intercourse was initiated by God (Gen. 1:27-28). It wasn't an afterthought. I remember at Youth for Christ meetings when I was a teen-ager, they used to have seminars on sexuality. One of the statements made was that "God designed sex so beautifully. He made it perfect, right down to the plumbing." Marriage and sex were given by God to man before sin entered the race. It's not an "accommodation" from God, but part of his original plan (Gen. 1:27 & 28). Sex is more than just a physical act, it is a symbol of the complete oneness of two persons joined together. That is why it is so very, very sacred and not to be used or taken lightly, as is (oftentimes) done in our generation. There is absolutely nothing to be ashamed of in sexual, marital relationships. It is a beautiful experience between a husband and wife (Gen. 1:31). The curse of the fall did not alter the sex act nor the basic desires which it satisfies. The sexual instinct is a primary drive created by God, but is to be used solely within an exclusive marital relationship (Gen. 3:16).

Naturally children are a normal, but not the exclusive, purpose of sexual relations. Sex provides the possibility of parenthood, which shows that one of the purposes of sexual intercourse is procreation (Gen. 1:27-28). But sex also provides an expression of mutual love with the primary purpose of giving and receiving pleasure as presented in Gen. 2:20-25. There is much more that the Old Testament talks about in regards to sexual relationships. Much can be found in the book of the Song of Solomon, the book of Proverbs and other places where the beauty, the wonder of sexual relationships and marital love as a whole are described in detail.

THE DEGENERATION

Sadly, the state of marriage and family, especially as seen in the treatment of women and children, degenerated over time. By the time of Christ, marriage was still covenantal, but the covenant could be easily broken (by the husband). The status of women was similar to that of a prized cow in the eyes of many religious leaders.

Children were raised to fulfill specific roles, where boys had significantly greater opportunity for learning and choice. Most girls/women had none. This was the world Jesus came to. But, as we will see, through Christ' teaching and sacrifice, all was turned upside right…for those who fully embrace his teaching.

JESUS' TEACHINGS ON MARRIAGE

Jesus established norms for his followers both by what he said and certainly by what he did. In the gospels, discussion of marriage, adultery, divorce, and remarriage is concentrated in several chapters (Matt. 5:19; Mk. 10:12; Luke 16:18, 20:27ff). Let's look at the several major areas of discussion that Jesus had regarding marriage.

MARRIAGE IN THE KINGDOM

Jesus placed marriage in proper perspective by emphasizing the primary importance of God's rule: *"Seek first his Kingdom and his righteousness, and all these things shall be yours as well"* (Matt. 6:33). Love within the family must be subordinated to the King's claim (Luke 14:26). To deify marriage is to destroy all chances that it might be Christian. *"I have married a wife"* (Luke 14:20) is no excuse for neglecting Christ's call. Co-dependency in marriage is in part a placing of one's spouse above God, a true form of idolatry. Believers may suffer loss of mates and homes for His sake (Matt. 19:29). Nevertheless, Christ enriches not only the kingdom's values, but it fills and enriches every dimension of life, including our wedded life.

THE NATURE OF MARRIAGE

One cannot understand the issues of divorce until he understands human nature and the Creator's plan for marriage, Jesus said, *NAS "Have you not read that He who made them from the beginning made them male and female"* (Matt. 19:4; also Mk. 10:6). The differentiation and mutuality of the sexes are part of man's make-up. Male and female were created to complement and complete each other in marriage and in community. Marriage gives expression to this original intent. *"For this reason a man shall leave his father and mother and be joined to his wife, and the two shall become one. So they are no longer two but one"* (Matt. 19:5-6a; Mk. 10:7f). Affirming truths long accepted in the covenant community, Jesus indicates that marriage requires the maturity to leave ones household to risk founding another. As stated earlier, one of the major difficulties for new marriages occur when one of the couple or both are unable to adequately separate or leave the family of origin. When they cannot do so it becomes impossible for them to adequately cleave to their spouse, let alone to become one flesh. Marriage means to assume the responsibilities of husband and wife, to covenant with each other before God, to embark upon a lifetime of self-giving (agape). In Hebraic parallelism, Jesus stresses the unity of two who consummate their marriage. The one flesh concept central to His thought may be seen as both real and ideal. It suggests a reality which couples experience, yet something towards which they strive as long as they live.

ON DIVORCE

On the basis of God's design, Jesus opposed the practice of divorce. "What therefore God has joined together, let no man put asunder" (Matt. 19:6b; Mk. 10:9). For Christians, marriage is never simply a social institution or a civil contract. It is a sacred union formed by God. The two are one before God. Divorce may occur but it is not in God's intent. Conscious of the Judaic debate on divorce, Jesus' listeners asked: "Why then did Moses command one to give a certificate of divorce, and to put her away?" (Matt. 19:7; also Mk. 10:3f). Jesus insisted that while Moses permitted divorce, he had not advocated it. Moses was curbing the practice of depriving a wife of her rights through desertion and of switching back to a former wife after her remarriage to someone else. He sought a remedy where sin had worked havoc. Of this Jesus says, "For your hardness of heart Moses allowed you to divorce your wives, but from the beginning it was not so" (Matt. 19:8; Mk. 10:5). It is one thing to recognize the existence of human failure; it is another to sanction it. Jesus insisted that the design of creation had precedence over the Mosaic concession.

Most significant is Jesus' declaration, "And I say to you: Whoever divorces his wife, except for unchastity, and marries another, commits adultery" (Matt. 19:9; compare to Mk. 10:11f; Luke 16:18. The exceptive clause is found in variant form in Matt. 5:31f). Only in Matthew 19:9 do we have the exceptive clause and the remarriage clause coordinated. The primary thrust of the verse is Jesus ruling on divorce. Here Jesus abolishes every other ground for divorce permitted in Mosaic provisions and Jewish practice except adultery (porneo - unchastity, fornication, illicit sexual intercourse). Jesus is especially hard on the man or woman (Mk. 10:12) who divorces the partner in order to marry another. This is labeled adultery, a sin against one's spouse and a sin against God. This enlarged understanding of adultery bids us not to define it simply as sexual infidelity.

Jesus recognizes then but one basis for divorce. While divorce is permissible, it is not obligatory. A strict interpretation of Jesus' words might tolerate divorce only where there has been sexual infidelity. However, a broader understanding of adultery would include other expressions of unfaithfulness and covenant breaking. Adulterous attitudes (Matt. 5:27f) and certain acts of non-sexual infidelity can also violate and kill a union (thus Paul's reference to desertion in I Cor. 7:15 is included under Jesus' exception). Yet one must beware of missing the intent of Jesus' words. He does not allow for an open-ended list of reasons for divorce as one's culture or times may dictate. He calls for determined, covenantal fidelity even where adultery has occurred. Jesus' words might have appeared harsh had we no furthermore indication of his ministry of forgiveness, but such is not the case.

* For a more thorough study on this topic see Dr. Chant's work, "The Corinthians", referenced in the back of this book.

JESUS' MINISTRY OF FORGIVENESS

Sin must not be magnified so as to obscure our common need for grace. Knowing the reality of their own sins, all Christians should be humbled by Jesus' words (Matt. 5:21-30). Nowhere is the compassion of Jesus more evident than when he deals with those broken by sexual sin. Noteworthy is His attitude towards the woman of Sychar, whose marital failures and adulterous situation had left her empty. By restoring her relationship to the Father, Jesus laid the basis for renewing all of her relationships (Jn. 4).
Confronted by a woman taken in adultery, Jesus ruled out the death penalty and offered God's grace. He forgave and urged her to sin no more (Jn. 8:1-11). His actions disclose understanding of the widespread problems men and women face. His forgiveness provides the basis for a fresh start. Where sin and guilt are confessed, healing can begin. Every person caught in the snares of adultery, marital discord, or divorce is redeemable. No sinner stands beyond Christ's reach. Disciples are called to seek forgiveness for their own failures and to minister the gospel of forgiveness and reconciliation to others (Luke 7:36-50; Matt. 18:15-22).

Jesus nowhere suggests that forgiveness should be denied to divorced persons nor that remarriage should be denied to those who have experienced His forgiveness.[4]

MARRIAGE AS VOCATION

In spite of contemporary attempts to abolish marriage as we know it marriage will undoubtedly continue throughout history (Matt. 24:38; Luke 17:27). Yet, it remains a temporal, not eternal, institution (Matt. 22:23-30; Mk. 12:18-25; Luke 20:27-36). Like the Sabbath, marriage was made for the benefit of mankind and not the reverse. To exaggerate its merit to the point of making it imperative for the full development of persons is a mistake. Although marriage is a holy calling, it is not for all. Jesus spoke of marriage as a vocation, stressing the disciples' choice in the matter. Christians may prefer to remain single for legitimate reasons (Matt. 19:10-12). To the suggestion that celibacy might be preferred, Jesus responded, "Not all men can receive this precept, but only those to whom it is given" (Matt. 19:11). In other words, most disciples will choose to marry. Most of us choose to marry with great delight. With Christ, either married or single life can be a beautiful venture.

Discussion of marriage, divorce, and remarriage is closely related to questions about family and children (Matt. 19:13-15; 18:1-6). It is a terrible thing for any adult to lead a child into a life of sin or who restricts entrance of a child into the Kingdom of Heaven. Those who choose to marry should be prepared to be responsible parents who will

---

[4] And hopefully, learned from the inevitable mistakes made, owned or accepted ones responsibility for the failure, and gained God's perspective on the areas of sin and repented.

nurture their children in the Christian walk. Even where a marriage is broken, this duty still remains. This high obligation should condition any discussion of divorce and remarriage.

Marriage is a vocation, yet most of the time we do not train people, nor do we require education on what marriage is or how to navigate it successfully. It is the Church's responsibility to train believers in all areas of the Christian walk. Marriage and family life is one of the most critical areas of training that believers and especially Christian leaders should be engaged in.

MARRIAGE AND FAMILY IN THE EARLY CHURCH

In the New Testament Church, marriage and family relationships were given high priority. In this section we study three primary aspects of marriage and family life as found in the early church.

AN APOSTOLIC VOICE

The first century world abounded with proponents of new ethics, marital experimentation, and sexual freedom. We in Western culture naively believe we have created something new with the sexual revolution; that certainly is not so. The Christian view of marriage caught on at Antioch, Ephesus, Corinth, and Rome. The greatness of the early church is illustrated through its uncompromising model of life in general, and marriage in particular, rather than an ethic of accommodation, as normally seen in the Roman Empire. The prophetic voice in a pagan world provided a new ideal of marriage and family. The church insisted that marriage was a holy estate in which partners were accountable to God and to each other so long as they lived (Rom. 1-4).

Christians exhibited a quality of love in marriage as well as in congregational life. There's a lofty ideal. *"Let marriage be held in honor among all, and let the marriage bed be undefiled; for God will judge the immoral and adulterous"* (Heb. 13:4). Congregations worked for these goals and called members to be accountable. Immorality was identified for what it was. Those afflicted by sin were called to repent and to reshape their lives after Christ's Word. Where this was not forthcoming, disciplinary action was exercised for the sake of the parties concerned, and for the sake of the church's life and witness (I Cor. 5:1f). Apostolic exhortation was anything but permissive (I Cor. 6:9-11). Persistence in sexual deviation or in marital discord was viewed as incompatible with life in the Kingdom. Yet the church was not recriminatory in spirit. Grace abounded as believers acknowledge Christ's forgiveness. Sin-broken persons were being transformed and so were their marriages (I Cor. 6:9ff; Eph. 2:1ff). This was an ongoing discipleship process in the early church.

APPLICATION OF THE GOSPEL

Under the leading of the Holy Spirit, the early church found itself with the task of working on the implications of Jesus' teaching in new situations. It engaged both in proclaiming its view of marriage to a troubled world and in problem solving, in behalf of those troubled with marital discord. The challenge was to apply the gospel without surrender to the spirit of the times. There are several passages of scripture that relate specifically to marriage and the family. Each will be discussed here. We begin with Paul's letter to Corinth, which provides many examples of the endeavor of the early church to grapple with difficult issues. We begin with I Cor. 7;

"Now concerning the things about which ye wrote unto me, it is good for a man not to touch a woman. Nevertheless, to avoid fornication, let every man have his own wife, and let every woman have her own husband. Let the husband render unto the wife her due; and likewise also, the wife unto the husband. The wife hath not power of her own body, but the husband; and likewise also the husband hath not power of his own body, but the wife. Defraud ye not one the other, except it be with consent for a time, that ye may give yourselves to fasting and prayer; and come together again, that Satan tempt you not for your incontinency. But I speak this by permission, and not by commandment. For I would that all men were even as I myself. But every man hath his proper gift of God, one after this manner, and another after that. I say, therefore, to the unmarried and widows, It is good for them if they abide even as I But if they cannot have self-control, let them marry; for it is better to marry than to burn. And unto the married I command, yet not I, but the Lord, Let not the wife depart from her husband; But and if she depart, let her remain unmarried, or be reconciled to her husband; and let not the husband put away his wife. But to the rest speak I, not the Lord, if any brother hast a wife that believeth not, and she be pleased to dwell with him, let him not put her away. And the woman who hath an husband that believeth not, and if he be pleased to dwell with her, let her not leave him. For the unbelieving husband is sanctified by the wife, and the wife is sanctified by the husband; else were your children

unclean, but now are they holy. But if the unbelieving depart, let him depart. A brother or a sister is not under bondage in such cases; but God hath called us to peace. For what knowest thou, O wife, whether thou shalt save thy husband? Or how knowest thou, O man, whether thou shalt save thy wife? But as God hath distributed to every man, as the Lord hath called every one, so let him walk. And so ordain I in all churches. Is any man called being circumcised? Let him not become uncircumcised. Is any called in uncircumcision? Let him not be circumcised. Circumcision is nothing, and uncircumcision is nothing, but the keeping of the commandments of God. Let every man abide in the same calling in which he was called. Art thou called, being a servant? Care not for it; but if thou mayest be made free, use it rather. For he that is called in the Lord, being a servant, is the Lord's freeman; likewise also he that is called, being free, is Christ's servant. Ye are bought with a price; be not ye the servants of men. Brethren, let every man, in whatever state he is called, there abide with God. Now concerning virgins, I have no commandment of the Lord; yet I give my judgment, as one that hath obtained mercy of the Lord to be faithful. I suppose, therefore, that this is good for the present distress, I say, that it is good for a man so to be. Are thou bound to a wife? Seek not to be loosed. Art thou loosed from a wife? Seek not a wife. But and if thou marry, thou hast not sinned; and if a virgin marry, she hath not sinned. Nevertheless, such shall have trouble in the flesh; but I spare you. But this I say, brethren, the time is short; it remaineth that both they that have wives be as though they had none; and they that weep, as though they wept not; and they that rejoice, as though they rejoiced not; and they that buy, as though they possessed not; And they that use this world, as not abusing it; for the fashion of this world passeth away. But I would have you without care. He that is unmarried careth for the things that belong to the Lord, how he may please the Lord; But he that is married careth for the things that are of the world, how he may please his wife. There is difference also between a wife and a virgin. The unmarried woman careth for the things of the Lord, that she may be holy both and in spirit; but she that is married careth for the things of the world, how she may please her husband. And this I speak for your own profit; not that I may cast a snare upon you, but for that which is seemly, and that ye may attend upon the Lord without distraction. But if any man think that he behaveth himself unseemly toward his virgin, if she pass the flower of her age, and need so require, let him do what he will, he sinneth not; let them marry. Nevertheless, he that standeth steadfast in his heart, having no necessity, but hath power over his own will, and hath so decreed in his heart that he will keep his virgin, doeth well. So, then, he that giveth her in marriage doeth well; but he that giveth her not in marriage doeth better. The wife is bound by the law as long as her husband liveth; but if her husband be dead, she is at liberty to be married to whom she will, only in the Lord. But she is happier if she so

> *abide, after my judgment; and I think also that I*
> *have the Spirit of God.*"

As can be clearly elucidated in any good commentary of the letter to the Corinthians, Paul is writing in response to a report given and a letter received, requesting response to several problematic issues facing the church. Paul counters those forbidding marriage and advocating celibacy. Marriage and its sexual dimensions are to be acknowledged as God's gifts. Marital love involves responsible caring for each other, self-control (not prolonged continence), and self-giving (I Cor. 7:1-7; also cf. I Tim. 4:1-3).

Single persons and widows may remain single if they desire to do so (which Paul prefers). They may also marry or remarry.[5] Whatever the case, love in a mutual sharing with another and not lust must prevail (I Cor. 7:8f). Elsewhere he advises young widows to remarry, apparently to keep busy and productive (I Tim. 5:11-14).

Acknowledging Christ's command, Paul advises against divorce where both are Christians (I Cor. 7:10 and 11b). Paul also discusses what should be done if separation or divorce does occur. He personally thinks that reconciliation should be attempted and where that fails, members should remain single (I Cor. 7:11a).

In a mixed marriage (one between a believer and unbeliever) the union should continue as long as the unbeliever consents. The believer should not initiate separation. If the unbeliever leaves, the believer "is not bound" to the marriage vow. Paul apparently held that

---

[5] For more on the Corinthian problem, see Dr. Ken Chant's previously referenced book.

desertion is comparable to the unfaithfulness of adultery. Desertion by the unbeliever can thus end a union. Yet as long as the union endures, the believing mate can be used of God to reach the other and to consecrate the children or bring them into a saving relationship with Jesus Christ (I Cor. 7:12-16).

The above illustrations reveal that God was richly at work in and through the early church. The church operated on the basis of the Apostolic Word. When the Word spoke to a given situation, it was applied with firmness. Where the particular problem was not expressly covered, the church prayerfully sought the Spirit's guidance. This precedent remains valid today.

INSTRUCTION REGARDING MARRIAGE AND THE FAMILY

The early church apparently felt it necessary to embark upon a program of instruction concerning sex, marriage, and family for the non-Hebrew believers. The New Testament letters contain such a body of teaching materials: I Cor. 11-14; Eph. 5:21-33; 6:1-4; Col. 3:18-25, I Tim. 3:1-13; 5:1-16; Titus 2:1-8; I Peter 3:1-9. This was to be taught by elders, teachers, pastors, and parents. Church leaders were also expected to exemplify these standards in their households (I Tim. 3:2-5). A brief survey will disclose the substance of these teachings.

All relationships, especially the marital relationship, must begin and be maintained in light of covenant. Our God is a covenant making and keeping God. He has covenanted with mankind to be our God with blessings flowing to the keepers of His covenant. Where the violation of covenant occurs, subsequent curses are assigned. (Deut. 27, 28)

In marriage, love was to follow after the covenant was established. That is, because of the commitment made in front of the covenant community, a commitment of faith and love would naturally emerge. The marriage covenant or agreement is of paramount importance in the life of believers and in the purposes of God.

There is order and beauty in God's creative plan which includes family and congregational life (I Cor. 11-14; I Peter 3). Paul and Peter saw this order in creation as providing sense and stability for life. Differentiation of the roles of husbands and wives (I Cor. 11:3; I Peter 3:1) in no way diminishes the equality of male and female before God (Gal. 3:28). Each person has unique gifts. Interdependence of members is desirable in both church and home.

The most excellent way of love (agape) transforms Christian marriage as well as the rest of life (I Cor. 13). Love is the key to right-relatedness, the end for which men and women were created. The capacity to love is a gift from God and not inherent in man. Deep in the human heart is a longing which will not be satisfied until the love of God is expressed in all relationships.

Explicit instruction is offered regarding the relationships of husbands and wives, parents and children, single members, orphans and widows so that all members might understand their responsibilities and privileges in family living (Eph. 5:21-6:4; Col. 3:18-25; I Tim. 3:1-13; 5:1-16; Titus 2:1-8; Heb. 13:4; James 1:27; I Peter 3:1-9). It is understood that love for Christ and for each other is the determinative force in Christian marriage and family life. The overriding emphases are mutuality, reciprocity, and love which seeks the development of the other's potential.

Members of Christian families are *"joint heirs of the grace of life"* (I Peter 3:7). A review of the major points found in these scriptures will expand and illuminate the subject, and follow below.

These instructions are still valid. Love and fidelity are to be learned from Christ through the Word. Respect for persons, appreciation for one's sexuality, the beauty of chastity before and in marriage, grace in dealing with human failure are to be learned within the context of the covenant people. There is little doubt that the quality and hope of life for future generations is dependent on the continuation of the Christian family. A positive educational approach must exist in every congregation and home if great ill is to be avoided, and if true human maturity is to be attained.

EXPANDED VIEW – THE KINGDOM PERSPECTIVE

Earlier in this book was presented the fall of man and the subsequent damage that was done to the relationship between the husband and wife. Priorities established by God in the garden, indicating the purpose for us all, were distorted through sin. Each blamed others (the man God and the woman, the woman the devil), and enmity was developed between them. Yet, God's Kingdom purpose (to be fruitful, multiply and have dominion over all God's creation, besides each other) was never changed. Through the cross, as members of God's Kingdom, all men and women have the potential to fulfill God's mandate for us.

PAUL'S PERSPECTIVE

Probably the most important, and perhaps most over referenced scripture of Paul's as it is related to marriage and family life is Ephesians 5:21-33 and 6:1-4, (paralleled in Col. 3:18-25). Vital principles that effect marital and family life are found here (though I would begin Paul's thoughts on the subject at Eph. 5:1). In context, Paul was less concerned about marriage as an institution (except by way of analogy) as he was for the harmonious functioning of Christ' church. Nonetheless, the principles are important, worthy of elucidation, and in light of our discussion on the Kingdom of God, most germane.

As previously presented, the fall of man produced almost unimaginable chaos, affecting all areas of life, not the least of which was life in the family. From Paul's perspective, all that was lost in the fall *is* restored in Christ (howbeit, rarely fully appropriated). Thus, for the Spirit empowered believer, the normal Christian should be able to live life as God intended, "from the beginning", including in our marriages and family.

Further, in the letter to the Ephesians, the crown jewel of Paul's writing and teaching ministry, Paul presents principles which should be manifested in the life of a family, and which would be a supreme example of Christ' Kingdom come to the earth for all to see.

IT TAKES IMITATION

"be imitators of God, as beloved Children." (Eph. 5:1)

This is no small task as a believer, to imitate God, unless we do so with a child like (innocent, without reservation) faith in God, His goodness and His word. This instruction from Paul was not for individuals alone, but can certainly apply to couples and the Christian community at large.

When we begin a relationship, it requires faith (not blind faith, but trust in God or another), and with a genuine willingness to enter the relationship with an open heart, imitating God's love toward each other in the relationship. To imitate God means to "walk in love (agape) just as Christ also gave himself up for us (v 2). Of courses, agape love speaks of a mature, unselfish love, which is not natural for humans and is rarely present in the beginning of a relationship; yet required to fulfill our purpose in Christ.

Much of the next 19 verses of Eph. 5 are also remarkably applicable to couples, but especially verse 21, which states "and be subject to one another in the fear (out of respect) of Christ." The highest submission is submission to God, to be followed by mutual submission in relationships (including marriage). Another view of this is that couples should be willing to submit (show and demonstrate respect, along with deference towards one another) in areas of gift and ability, not based upon gender or other external attributes. To do so shows maturity in relationship and give honor to Christ and his word.

Following these important versus is Paul's instructions regarding marriage and family as a picture of the church. Marriage should fits show mutual respect, while effectively meeting the needs of most women (love) and men (respect), to essential elements of an effective and happy marriage.

This last part is summarized in Eph. 5:33,

"Nevertheless, let each individual among you (men) also love (agape) his own life even as himself, and let the wife see to it that she respect her husband."

This theme, love and respect, is also seen in Paul's other writings (Col 3; 1 Cor 7) or at least assumed. It is also the focus of a fairly recent book by Emerson Eggerich titled "Love and Respect". In his work he sites the 20 year study of 2000 couples that give evidence that love and respect are foundational ingredients to a happy and successful marriage.[6]

Wives need to know they are loved, really loved by their husbands. When they feel unloved, they internalize it as hurt, often reacting in criticism towards their husband. The average husband will most often respond to criticism with withdrawal, experiencing the criticism as a lack of respect. This cycle, often seen in dysfunctional and "normal" marriages, demonstrates the continual effect of the Fall and sin in the lives of even God's people. Husbands that learn to love (demonstrated in a way that is sensible and understood by the wife) and when the wife respects (not worship, but attempts to affirm and bless) her husband, it shows that God's Kingdom rule has come to this marriage. Of course, since the marriage is foundational to the family, when love and respect in harmonious balance are seen in marriage, the children of that union will have greater opportunity to grow as God intended.

AND BABY MAKES THREE

If godly principles of love and respect are lived out in the home, a couple should rightly expect that obedient children (12 years of age and under obey) and honoring young people (age 13 or so and above) should ensue, creating a well ordered, God honoring home. Perfect, never; but

---

[6] Study by John Gottman from "Why Marriages Succeed or Fail."

moving in the right direction by the grace of our wonderful God.

PETER'S PRINCIPLES

Peter the apostle addressed the issue of marriage in his writing as well. We read in 1 Pe. 3:1-7;

"1 In the same way, (as previously stated in previous versus, which discuss Christ' willingness to submit himself to the cross for us) you wives, be submissive

(subject, show respect) to your own husbands so that even if any of them are disobedient to the word, they may be won without a word by the behavior of their wives. 2 as they observe your chaste and respectful behavior. 3 And let not your adornment be merely external-braiding the hair, and wearing gold jewelry, and putting on dresses; 4 but let it be the hidden person of the heart, with the imperishable quality of a gentle and quiet spirit, which is precious in the sight of God. 5 For in this way in former times he holy women also, who hoped in God, used to adorn themselves, being submissive to their own husbands. 6 Thus Sarah obeyed Abraham, calling him lord, and you have become her children if you do what is right without being frightened by any fear. 7 You husbands likewise live with your wives in an understanding way, as with a weaker vessel, shine she is a woman; and grant her honor as a fellow-heir of the grace of life, so that your prayers may not be hindered."

As the reader can no doubt see, Peter addresses the issue in a similar manner as Paul, with similar assumptions (maturity, believers, etc.), but presents some additional insights. These insights are helpful to our understanding of God's perspective on healthy marriages.[7]

Peter begins with the biblical teaching of submission on the part of the wife to the husband. Again, this may be the least popular and most misunderstood concept in society today. The bible does not teach the general suppression of women under men. Nor does the principle of submission require a woman to become a subservient. Further, it must be noted that submission does not in any way mean inferiority. Both the man and the woman have equal value and standing as God's children. One is not superior to the other, excepting in areas of obvious gifting. Remember, here is equality in Christ (Gal 3:28), Thus there is to be mutual submission to each other, and one key to submission is humility (see Phil. 2:3-4). Finally, submission has its limits in marriage. Where there is unrepented sexual immorality, physical or sexual abuse, etc., the disillusionment of the marriage may be recommended, even required.

It also must be noted that in context of Peter's teaching was the very common reality of a common problem (in that day) which was a divided home. This marital situation, where the wife had become a Christian and her husband remained a non-believer presented a dicey situation at best (as it does today).

> "When a Christian wife interacted with an unbelieving husband, she needed to be submissive according to cultural norms in order to save her

[7] The author gratefully acknowledges the excellent teaching notes provided by George Stahnke of Renewal Ministries of Colorado Springs (www.renewalcs.org), which were used as the basis for this section.

marriage and sometimes even her life. But she ought not participate in her husband's pagan religion or submit to actions that dishonored God...Submission does not mean inferiority or blind obedience. A wife who accepts her husband's authority is accepting the relationship that God has designed and giving her husband leadership and responsibility." (Life Application Bible Commentary)

The reason for such submission is the fact that a woman's words alone will not persuade the average husband. It is necessary to be an example to soften the heart of a non-believing husband.

AN EXAMPLE

After my mother was born again, she became a true, passionate, faithful and unfortunately belligerent preacher to my father. My dad, a good guy but with much insecurity and a short fuse, would argue weakly with my mom about all the time she spent with "Jesus and that church". Almost every Sunday, after church, my mom with great sincerity would return home to "share" the message of the week. This antagonized my dad mercilessly. She genuinely wanted him to experience Christ, but her method was as subtle as a brick through a plate glass window.

One day my mom simply "quit". In her words, she "gave up on him", and started to love him, spend time with my dad, even stay home from church at times to be with him. A year or so after the change, my dad showed up at church. Soon thereafter, he made a decision for Christ.

One day I asked my dad why he suddenly began to come to

church. He related the story shared here, but with a twist. He stated "when your mom stopped yelling and began to treat me well, I assumed she must have really gotten saved... so I had to check it out for myself."

Well, if such a demeanor of respect (submission) will work to change an unbelievers heart, (at least potentially), how much more should it touch the heart of a believing husband who is open (hopefully) to the prompting of the Holy Spirit, a sanctified conscience and the Word of God.

Of course, a one way street was never God's intention. Peter admonishes men to both love heir wives and to understand them (no small task). This indicates that a husband, in order to love his wife, should listen well enough and become fascinated enough with his wife to know her needs (not necessarily what she wants) with a willingness to sacrifice for her benefit. Thus, every husband should make Christ's love for the church the pattern for loving his wife. Christ willingly sacrificed for the church his very life, and husbands in like manner should be willing to sacrifice, in more than just work, their life for their wife. A husband does this as he tenderly works with his wife, encouraging her growth in her God given strengths and talents.

Finally, husbands are to honor protect and provide for their wives and families, to the best of their abilities, as God gives strength.

Thus, Peter gives hope to the wife of an unbelieving husband, for he may be won over to Christ. It is not by her compelling arguments or nagging words, but by her loving and respectful behavior that she just might make an impact on an unbelieving husband.

In conclusion, the two sides of the marriage coin are love and respect. The more a wife respects her husband in word and deed, and the more a husband genuinely and with understanding loves his wife, he happier and more fulfilled the marriage and family will be.

GOD'S PLAN FOR HUSBANDS AND WIVES

DISCUSSION POINTS

1. Use these agree/disagree statements to think about marriage.

- Love means never having to say you are sorry
- Commitment is more important than love in marriage
- I can change what I don't like in my spouse.
- I cannot expect marriage to make me happy
- Marriage is a 50-50 relationship

2. Since God's plan for husbands is modeled after His relationship with His creation, discuss what we know about God and His character. List your responses, and relate them to marriage values.

3. Children develop their God-concept through the modeling of their fathers. If a child's father is loving, gentle, compassionate and strong, the child will see God as having similar traits. If a child's father is harsh, demanding and emotionally distant, what will the likely results be? Discuss this.

MARRIAGE IN THE WEST

As an indicator of what is actually happening in Western nations, one should learn from history and statistics that give us a better picture of our modern world. Furthermore, as we review these facts, we will attempt to integrate these statistics into the context of the God's will and purpose.

In 1870 the divorce rate in the U.S. was 3 for every 1000 marriages. In 1960, 26 out of every 100 marriages ended in divorce. By 1975 it was 42 of every 100 and by the year 2000 there was a divorce rate of between 55 and 61 of every 100 marriages.

The U.S. Department of Labor statistics indicated that in 1974 there were 2,223,000 marriage licenses applied for in the United States compared to 1,970,000 divorces granted in the same year. In November, 1974, an article in the Los Angeles Times indicated that in Orange County, California during the first six months of 1974 there were 6,372 marriages, and 6,702 divorces. This same trend is evidenced even in King County, Washington State, a somewhat conservative and less populated area: in the entire year of 1975 there were 11,558 marriage licenses applied for in contrast of 11,599 dissolution's applied for - that is 41 more dissolution's applied for than marriages!

Figures on divorce may or may not be meaningful in isolation. One of the implications of these figures, according to the U.S. News and World Report article cited earlier, is that there will be more conglomerate families. At this time, **more than 30% of school-age children** are living with parents who have been divorced at least once. In addition, perhaps one-fifth of **all U.S. children under 18 currently live in single-parent families**. These statistics are alarming but they are even higher in different cultural systems; especially Black and Hispanic family systems where racism and poverty are issues that must be overcome.

Cause and effect relationships are difficult to trace, but when indicators of conflict, aggression, crime and emotional insecurity rise, we can reasonably assume that personal and family fulfillment will be on the decline. Further, at least **one million** young Americans, most of them from middle-class homes, **run away** from home each year.

Suicide is said to be the second leading cause of death for young Americans between the ages of 15 and 24. Again, one cannot absolutely argue that the increasing divorce rate is causing children to run away or to commit suicide, but the figures strongly suggest that familial dissatisfaction is present.

It has also been noted that one out of nine youths in American society ends up in juvenile court by age 18 and that approximately 10% of all school-age children have moderate to severe mental and emotional problems. The personal trauma, tragedy, and devastation described by these statistics are only part of the total loss sustained by our society. To further exacerbate the current trends, there continues to be a high rate of child abuse and domestic violence within our society. When the unfulfilled personal potential going to waste is estimated, the true cost of current trends of family life deterioration in The West are greatly increased.

ALTERNATIVES

In light of these statistics, and others that could be presented, we are faced with at least two alternatives.

One alternative is to assume that the whole question of the family is problematic and, in light of the current figures, look for different, alternative ways to cope and learn to live together. In short, we must assume that the traditional family institution has been found wanting and ineffective: thus new alternatives must be explored and tried.

The other alternative is to suggest that the institution of the family has not been found at fault, **but man's application and approach to the family has been faulty**. We still believe that there are viable, important components to the Biblical perspective on marriage and the family, and that the reason marriages are in trouble is because these have not been absolutely and consistently applied - not because there is a defect in the basic model itself. We know for a fact, as Christians, that God's primary intention for marriage and family as presented in the Old and New Testament is the same model for us today.

The problem is not with the institution of marriage; the problem focuses more on the individuals within that structure and their attitudes toward marriage and values. The focus of the church must shift from denial of the problem or counseling to attempt restoration, to a biblically mandated teaching and training on family life that is preventative in nature. Our only hope is to rebuild the foundation of family life, which begins with the marriage relationship.

CHANGES IN FAMILY LIFE

CORE CHARACTERISTICS OF MARRIAGE

The core characteristics of marriage are those attitudes, beliefs and actions, which are intrinsic to the nature of a marital relationship. Many of these characteristics are culturally determined, and each culture is different and unique. If you will, core characteristics are constants; they are always present in this relationship, and they exert continuing and significant influences on each other, on the ways each partner interacts with the other, and on the development of their relationship.

The core characteristics effecting marriage include intellectual balance, religion, race, ethnic background and socioeconomic class. Each will be briefly explored.

INTELLECTUAL BALANCE

Whether covertly or overtly, consciously or unconsciously, each couple strikes some kind of intellectual balance between themselves. Family therapists will often relate this balancing to a system, in which all members of the family influence one another. Keeping an equilibrium or "homeostatic balance" is necessary for adequate family functioning. If a couple is approximately equal in intelligence and common sense, this kind of balance ordinarily tends to make the fewest "waves" between them. If, however, they are equal, but one of them has worries concerning masculine/feminine roles, then trouble may arise. For example, if the husband believes that a man should be smarter than his wife, he may waste much time and energy trying to prove to him, her, and others, that he is really smarter than she is.

If the wife has had instilled in her the concept that a woman should never appear as smart as a man, that a smart woman is not attractive to men, she may play down or belittle her intelligence and act less intelligent than she really is, especially when in public together. She may retreat into her "wifely" role and become, for example, super housekeeper and super homemaker, leaving the intellectual forum to him.

If one is smarter than the other, the more intelligent one may lord it over the less-able or may simply be him or herself and let things happen as they will. Or the more intelligent one may acknowledge his or her intellectual superiority but value the other's common sense or emotional perceptiveness.

Whatever intellectual balance exists, however, is less important than the way each (and both) of the partners react to and use the balance. These reactions and uses will depend, of course, on who each partner is, and their level of relative maturity.

RELIGION

Whatever the religious background and affiliation, each partner thinks, feels, acts, and interacts in relation to some religious position (even if it is a non-religious one of agnosticism or atheism) because every human being must in some way deal with certain moral, spiritual, and philosophical questions. For example, if both partners adhere to Biblical, orthodox religious beliefs, they are likely to see marriage as a forever commitment. Further, they will have strong rules against premarital and extramarital sex, and will be more likely to subscribe to a hierarchy of authority in relationship, whether patriarchal or matriarchal (which is much less common).

If the partners do not adhere to Orthodox Biblical beliefs, they are not as likely to consider marriage as a long term commitment and may feel freer to consider divorce as an alternative to an unsatisfactory relationship.

If the marital partners come from different religious backgrounds, then they may well face problems that affect their relationship. Suppose a Catholic and a Protestant marries. In some way they have to deal with the Catholic Church's stance on interfaith marriages. For example, if the couple is married in a civil ceremony only, then the Catholic Church does not consider them married in the eyes of God. Most certainly, that places some emotional burden on the Catholic partner and it may arouse resentment in the Non-Catholic spouse. If there are children, in whose faith will they be raised? If the Protestant partner insists on their being raised as Protestants, then the Catholic partner is penalized by his/her church. If the Catholic partner insists on a Catholic upbringing, then the Protestant partner may feel left out of the family, (as might the Catholic in reversed circumstances), and develop resentment or bitterness because of feeling pressure to bow to another faith's demands.

Again, the pressures exerted by the formal religion(s) and by outside factors (such as family and friends) can place great stresses on the marital relationship. These stresses and influences inevitably affect the lifestyle that the marriage develops. As was stated above, oftentimes couples will react to one another in similar fashion as they related to siblings and to mother and father in their family of origin. This can also be seen in areas of religion where certain family systems may have seen religion as important and vital and others as a lessor value. These are all topics that couples must be willing to look at and work through (preferably prior to commitment to marry) if they are going to have a successful and positive marriage experience.

One note of importance. Where cultural norms or patterns are in agreement with scripture, or at least not specifically forbidden, they can be helpful, productive and to be rejoiced in. However, when cultural characteristics are in conflict with the clear reading of scripture and its subsequent principles, core characteristics of cultural norms should, even must be modified in favor of God's word.

RACE

If the partners are of the same race, then the effects of this characteristic on the marital relationship are minimized. If the couple is from a racial minority, then any prejudices, stereotypes, and discrimination that are directed against that particular race obviously place strains on the marital relationship.

If the marriage is an interracial one, then special stresses may be placed on the relationship. For example, if a black and white marry, who will they mix with socially? Which race will accept their marriage? Where will they live? How will each of them handle whatever latent prejudices he or she may have? Should they inflict their interracial choice on children? Again, questions and potentially difficult situations cannot help but have an effect on the ways the partners interact and on the kind and quality of relationship they develop. Though we hope that these issues can be easily overcome within the Church of Jesus Christ, generally this is not the case. It is the Church's responsibility to love and accept people as they are. Unfortunately, the Church has a long, long way to go, especially in regards to race relations.

ETHNIC BACKGROUND

Ethnic background often has a strong influence on the roles and expectations of the partners. If both come from the same ethnic group and from families that have fairly similar degrees of adherence to that background, then each partner will hold essentially the same values and expectations, seeing the husband's and wife's roles in similar fashion.

For example, if each is from a fairly strict Italian, Polish or Puerto Rican family, then each will be used to certain stereotypical roles and expectations; the man is the head of the household, the woman is subservient to him; masculinity and femininity are rather rigidly defined; the husband holds a job, the wife bears and raises the children; and the family (the extended family) may more important than the individuals in any given marriage. Again, a couple must seriously consider the ethnic background, because although ethnic differences can be overcome, they can create difficult impediments to a healthy marriage.

SOCIOECONOMIC CLASS

Expectations that one spouse has of the other can be an area of great discord in marriage. This can often be seen when the marital partners come from divergent economic background. Extra care should be taken to establish clear and realistic expectations of one another to avoid unnecessary conflict caused by socioeconomic class differences. An individual entering marriage that was raised with a "silver spoon" in their mouth may not be adequately prepared for the realities of early marital life.

Certainly it becomes apparent that decisions for marriage should not be made on impulse based solely on "chemistry." Significant thought, prayer, and the seeking of wise counsel is not only highly advised but virtually essential if we are going to experience a successful marriage.

"Many a romance begins when you find the girl of your dreams, and ends when you wake up."
Unknown Source

FULFILLING NEEDS IN MARRIAGE

One of the motivating factors for marriage is the fulfillment of needs. It is admirable to say that we are marrying the other person in order to help him/her fulfill needs; but, to be perfectly honest, most individuals enter marriage with a deep need to have personal needs met in the relationship. In fact, there often tremendous, unconscious expectations placed on a partner; to not only meet some needs, but all needs, including deficiency needs created in the family of origin.

For example, when I was first married, I had an expectation of my wife in regards to the cleanliness of our home. I was raised in a family system where cleanliness was important and stressed. In my wife's home any horizontal surface that could be found in the house was made to be piled on (my perception, perhaps a "slight" exaggeration). In the beginning of our relationship, we had significant conflict over the cleanliness of the house because I had expectations which became immature, emotional demands. Of course, my wife had other expectations. This is not unusual, especially in the beginning of a marriage.

In marriage counseling, one of the major complaints couples raise is that of not having their needs met. Often one partner is attempting to meet the needs of the other, but he or she does not always know what the needs are, or does not know exactly how to meet them. In Appendix 1 of this book you will find a worksheet that will help you to begin to determine the basic needs you have within your marriage and what your spouse's needs may be. It would behoove a couple to take the time to complete this worksheet and to do the hard work of determining what your needs are, what your spouses needs are and what you can realistically do to fulfill them together.

A MATTER OF DEFINITION

It is important for a married person to define his or her needs specifically and then indicate how he or she would like their partner to respond in order to meet those needs. Some have asked, "Doesn't it take the romance out of marriage if you have to tell the other person exactly what you need?" Not at all. In fact, it can increase the romance, as now your spouse will not have to play the game of mind reading to figure out what you need, let alone what you want!

Years ago, a psychologist named Abraham Maslow suggested that each person has certain basic needs in life. He listed these needs in order of importance or as a hierarchy. First, a person seeks to fulfill his physiological needs. These are those things that are necessary in order to sustain life: food, water, oxygen, rest, etc. Second, a person seeks to fulfill safety needs, which involve the need for a safe environment, protection from harm, etc. Third, after having the first two sets of needs fulfilled, a person seeks to fulfill his or her need for love and belonging. This includes a desire for affectionate relationships with others. Fourth, a person seeks to fulfill his or her need for esteem. Esteem involves receiving recognition as a worthwhile person. Finally, after the other levels of need are met, a person seeks to fulfill the need for actualization. This is the need to fulfill ones potential, to develop into a full, creative individual. In problem marriages, the needs of a the couple are neither bad or inappropriate, but rather the strategy they have for meeting their needs is not effective. Dr. Larry Crabb has written a book called "Effective Biblical Counseling", which describes this process in great detail. We often look to our spouse to meet all of our human, emotional needs. Often these are needs that have not been adequately met prior to marriage. When we seek to obtain from our spouse help, support, unconditional love, etc., which they are unable to provide fully, it leads to certain disappointment. This can create a syndrome of the blind leading the blind. If the blind leads the blind, will they not both fall into the pit? (Luke 6:39)

Most husbands and wives fulfill the first two levels of needs in each other (the physiological and safety needs). Most husbands, for example, allow their wives enough air, water, food and rest. Most are concerned about keeping the car in good running order, making sure the house is safe, with proper lighting, ventilation, locks, and so on. But where most husbands and wives fail, or at least struggle, is in meeting their spouse's need for love and belonging, esteem, and self-actualization. It is important to remember that no one human being has the capacity to meet all of the needs of another individual. We must have the power of God and his love shed abroad within our hearts and a positive relationship with Jesus Christ to be able to become the kind of person that God wants us to be.

There are four primary ways that we may attempt to fulfill our needs in marriage. Each are important but insufficient in meeting the needs of either marital partner. The first way is through status or "how important I am." Our self-image or self-concept is often built upon our appearance. In America especially, whether or not you are attractive and thin with fit physique is vitally important for some. How do I look, we ask ourselves? If our self-concept is built upon the external presentation, then as we grow older we will have difficulty maintaining a positive self-image. We must ask ourselves to what degree does our self-concept depend upon external, physical criteria?

A second attempt to meet our needs is through belonging or being wanted and accepted. Belonging rests on the voluntary attitude of others as they display their acceptance of us. It is a sense of security with others who love and accept us. Our spouse probably accepts us, but if we come into marriage with a sagging self-image, we may not be able to receive the acceptance provided.

The third way appears as worthiness, as seen in the statement; "I am good, I count." Worthiness rests on the introspective attitude of self-approval and being affirmed as a person of value. Again, if affirmation was readily provided in our family of origin, we will have an adequate supply upon entering marriage. However, deficiencies are often projected on our spouse as their unwillingness to supply what we so desperately need. A thoroughly unrealistic expectation.

Fourth is competence or the feeling of adequacy. Competence rests on the evaluations received, in part, through relationships and on one's present sense of success. When one feels adequate or competent, a sense of security is evident which leads to positive action. Where a sense of inadequacy exists, the opposite is generally seen.

These are some of the ways in which our society evaluates us as to whether or not we are worthwhile or important. Based upon our self-perception, we will attempt to fulfill our needs in marriage. God has a better way! Think about this. Your worth is so great, that if you had been the only person living on the earth, God would have sent his Son to die for you! You count that much to Him. Many of us strive so hard for a sense of adequacy. We may attempt to compensate through college degrees, or advanced employment, or even obtaining a coveted position within the local church in order to prove worth. God has declared us to be adequate in what he has done for us in His Son Jesus Christ. In Romans 5:8 states;

> "God commends his love toward us, in that, while
> we were yet sinners, Christ died for us."

Jesus would not have died for people that were not worth something. In fact, we were worth a great price. Our sense of adequacy and self-image as Christians is to be rooted in the person of Jesus Christ. We are worthwhile; we are OK human beings because of Christ living in us, having been adopted into the very family of God. (Rom. 8:15)

In your relationship with Father God you are assured of your belonging. In your relationship with the Son of God, you are assured of worthiness. In your relationship with the Holy Spirit, you have a secure sense of competence as He is our Comforter "Counselor", Guide and source of Strength.

Within most classification of needs, the word esteem or self-esteem arises. The concept of self-esteem or self-image is important to understanding foundationally in marriage. If one marries with a low self-esteem, a strain can be placed upon the marriage. You may have married in order to build your self-esteem or have sought to find a spouse to give a sense of meaning or worth. If you have questions about your worth, your value, your feelings about yourself, you may want to do some self exploration in light of precious discussion and God's word. It may further help to talk to someone who has the ability to help you understand yourself and to understand who you are in Christ. It is so important to know that we are special in God's eyes, worthwhile because he has redeemed us and adopted us into his eternal family.

"We do not deal much in facts when we are contemplating ourselves."
Mark Twain

MATURITY FOR MARRIAGE

It is difficult to know whether we are truly ready for marriage. To a great extent we are never ready and always getting ready. Provided below is a list of attitudes and attributes which will provide an idea of the positive and negative components to maturity and marital readiness. This is but a guide. As you read each one, it would be helpful to take an honest inventory of yourself, but please do not take an inventory of your spouse at the same time. We already have the Holy Spirit who is more than adequate to reveal to us the hidden places of our heart. We do not have to be the Holy Spirit for our mate.

THE MATURE PERSON

- He/she is not dominated by moods, and has learned constructive ways for working out feelings. He/she does not take out their feelings on others.
- He/she is cooperative. He/she does not have to dominate others.
- He/she has overcome tendencies towards jealousy.
- He/she is not easily hurt.
- He/she can be generous in their judgment of others and give them the benefit of the doubt.
- He/she works to be adaptable, and is able to adjust to differences or to changes that life brings.
- He/she has grown up to the point that they hold positive and wholesome attitudes about sex.
- A mature person is reasonably cautious about making decisions, not making major choices on impulse, or acting first and thinking later.
- Has learned functional ways of problem solving, while avoiding unhealthy or destructive escapes when under pressure.

- He/she is realistic about what can be expected from life and what they must give in return. They do not live in a "dream world."
- He/she has a fairly clear idea of what kind of person they are and hope to be.
- He/she can discipline themselves to meet responsibilities and obligations to others.
- He/she has learned to use good judgment in earning and spending money, and can plan their finances and stick to the plan.
- He/she is reasonably independent of his/her parents, yet not childishly rebellious toward them.
- He/she can sacrifice personal preferences when the good of another requires it.
- He/she works to overcome selfishness and self-centeredness.

Few of us may meet these requirements completely (though we may attempt to convince ourselves that we do.) You may want to develop a list of "areas for improvement" for yourself. The more mature we are as people, the better we are as potential and present marital partners. The one who is still childish in marriage, no matter how old they are in years, shows rather opposite characteristics than the ones listed previously. The reader is encouraged to do the same exercise as previously done, looking at each item while asking yourself the question, am I mature or immature, and what would God have me do about it?

THE IMMATURE PERSON

- He/she is inclined to be erratic and moody, and is likely to impose their moods upon others.

- He/she is competitive and aggressive in trying to have their own way. They tend to "cut down" or belittle others.
- He/she is jealous and easily hurt.
- He/she is rigid. They cannot admit their own mistakes and try to change, but must always be "right" and others wrong.
- He/she cannot put themselves in another's place and understand how the other person feels or why another thinks as they do.
- He/she does not face their problems constructively. Rather, they blame others for whatever happens to them. They use escapes such as temper tantrums, sulking, reckless driving, or other acting out, when things upset them.
- He/she make snap judgments and impulsive decisions without taking time to think a matter through or obtaining all the facts needed for making a wise decision.
- He/she cannot look ahead, but thinks only of immediate, self-focused needs. What they want and need is more important to them than the wishes or needs of anyone else. In their relationships with others, they do not adjust, but expect others to adjust to them and their ways.

An individual with a solid and Biblical sense of self will look more like the mature than the immature. All of us need to work toward maturity to be conformed to the image of Christ. Let's look furthermore at the issue of maturity from a Biblical perspective.

FURTHER MARKS OF MATURITY

In Ephesians 4:14-15 we read

"As a result, we should no longer be babes, tossed back and forth and carried here and there with every wind of teaching that springs from human craftiness and ingenuity for devising error; but, telling the truth in love, we should grow up in every way toward Him who is the Head-Christ."

Dr. Clyde M. Narramore has developed a list of characteristics of a mature person. They include:

- A mature person is realistic about him/herself, others, his or her talents and shortcomings. You will never be accepted by others until you accept yourself.
- A mature person is one who accepts frustrations with poise and humility.
- A mature person has the ability to cooperate with others. Not constantly seeking to win or be top dog, but willing to share and to be in a cooperative relationship with others.
- A mature person can use their talents and abilities effectively. Not just for their benefit but for the benefit of others as well.
- A mature person is capable of postponing a present pleasure for a future good. They are able to delay their gratification.
- A mature person can stand on their own two feet and make decisions for his/herself without constantly depending upon his/her spouse for support.

- A mature person can accept both praise and criticism with humility and poise. They are able to laugh at themselves and laugh along with others.
- A mature person does not expect perfection in others but is able to see that we are all doing the best we can to survive in this crazy world. We all have our own eloquent style of relating and therefore must be gracious and loving toward one another.
- A mature person is capable of loving someone else other than him/ herself.

It has been stated in many places that we live in an age of anxiety and narcissism (self-centeredness). The 1970's and early 1980's were justifiably characterized as the "me" generation (in most Western culture). Someone that is focused on themselves only is not a person of maturity as prescribed in the Word of God.

A person who lacks maturity is described by many verses in the Word of God. Some of these include a person demonstrating...

- Strife, bitter envying, confusion, evil work (Jam 3:14-16; 1 Cor. 3:3), or one who lacks the attribute of quietness and confidence (Isaiah 32:17). Further, a person who...
- Leans on the arm of the flesh or ones own strength and power rather than leaning on God for his strength and support (Jeremiah 17:5-6). Also, one who is...
- Easily offended (Psalm 119:165) and

- Will not call his sins by their proper names, but makes excuses for his actions - i.e., "I'm upset," "I'm moody," "I'm under tension," "I'm temperamental," "That person gives me a pain" or even worse, "The devil made me do it." It is further someone who...
- Feels he is not appreciated and people do not understand them. They take on the role of a victim. They also tend towards being...
- unable to discern blessing or good when it comes (Jeremiah 17:6), having
- A critical spirit, being ready to gossip (Proverbs 16:27-28, ef. Eph. 4:29) at a moments notice, always ready to justify themselves (Proverbs 12:15, 16:2), and
- Cannot accept frustration or disappointment, but has juvenile reactions when things do not go the way they want them to go (1 Cor. 13:11). They are a man or woman who must have their own way NOW: they cannot wait, and
- When criticized they become hostile or nasty; they cannot be realistic about themselves, nor are they able to...
- Forgive; in fact they enjoy keeping grudges (Ephesians 4:20-32). Thus, they
- Cannot practice love for their enemies or bless those who persecute them. (Mat 5:44, Romans 12:14, 1 Cor. 13:4-7), nor can they ever admit something when they are wrong. Finally, to say...
- "I'm sorry." is almost impossible.

It is quite obvious that who you are as a person and what expectations you may have been raised to believe are the primary determinants as to how well you will function in your marital relationship. Ultimately, what is being discussed in all this is the need to love. However...

WHAT IS LOVE?

In the Americanized view of marriage, the purpose and the reason for the institution of marriage is love. Yet, what is the meaning of this often over utilized word? In your own mind right now, you might want to complete this statement: "Love is _____." As you do some thinking about love, you might ask yourself the question, "what are the differences in the types of love? How is love defined? Someone has said, 'love is the insatiable desire to squeeze juice from a lemon." I'm not really sure what they meant, but someone thought it was important. This points out that sometimes our definitions of love may not fully make sense to others. For example: another possible definition is "that love is...a feeling that you feel when you feel that you felt that you feel a feeling that you've never felt before." OK, I'm glad we got that straight.

There are four Greek words that Scripture uses to describe what love is (see Ken Chant's, "Christian Life" for a full description). Those words are *eros*, which refers to physical, passionate or sexual love; *philio,* which covers the emotional aspect of love dealing with closeness, sharing, companionship, and building each other up; *storge,* which speaks of family love and loyalty, and *agape. Agape* is unconditional, spiritual love. It says, I love you whether you are lovely or unlovely. Agape love is characteristic of God's love for us.

Love is an art which requires four basic concepts. **First,** there must be ultimate attention given to the care of the other person. If you are going to love someone, the focus of your attention must be on that person, not on self or many people.

Secondly, there must be an emotional desire to assume responsibility for the emotional needs of the other person. We don't enter relationships by force. Certainly no one had to twist my arm for me to marry my wife. I married her because I loved her and I saw her as the most wonderful woman in the world for me. Because of that, I must assume a certain amount of responsibility for her care, nurture, and growth as a person. I am also aware that I cannot meet all of her needs in my own strength.

Thirdly, there must be the highest respect for the identity of the spouse as a total person within his or her own right. If we say we love our spouse but we put them down in public, or we treat them badly in front of our children, we are not showing them respect and ultimately do not love them.

The same holds true when we think of races and cultures. We can say we love them, but if we don't show them respect for who they are and for their differences, then our faith is dead because we do not have works which demonstrate it.

Fourthly, there must be a thorough knowledge of the person who is to be loved (J.A. Fritze). The more one knows their spouse, the more they are able to love them. Also, the more one needs to love because the imperfections easily seen are readily seen. That is the same for couples; the more the wife knows her husband, the more she sees the obvious imperfections, with the many faults and inconsistencies. A true and mature love is able to love someone that one knows intimately, while overlooking, even rejoicing in the failures and foibles of the individual. Love is truly an art that requires these four basic concepts to make it grow.

The importance of love cannot be minimized. Jesus said;

> *"I give you a new commandment; love one another as I have loved you. It is by this that everyone will recognize you as my disciple by your loving one another."* (John 13:35)

Love is commanded by our Lord, a command we must strive to obey. Paul again reminds us;

> *"Husbands, love your wives just as Christ loved the church and gave himself for it." Ephesians 5:25*
> *"...that they should teach what is right, so as to train the younger women to love their husbands and children, to be discrete, pure minded, domesticated, good women, ready to submit to their husbands in order that God's message may not be maligned." Titus 2:4-5*

Love is sacrificial. Love is sometimes difficult. To love someone that is being unlovely can be one of the most trying experiences for us, yet it is not something that is requested by God but rather something required by Him. What He requires of us, He will empower us to do.

LOVE MAKES A MARRIAGE GOOD

As briefly mentioned, there are four words for love. Each

provides an aspect of total love to be seen and practiced in a healthy marriage.

EROS

Eros is the love that seeks sensual expression. *Eros* is a romantic or sexual love. It is inspired by the biological structure of human beings which was created by God. The husband and wife in a good marriage will love each other romantically and erotically. Of course, this is to be done so with sensitivity and respect. Sex should never be used to coerce or punish, or be forced or manipulated (more on sex to follow).

PHILIO/STORGE

In a healthy marriage, the husband and wife are also friends. Friendship means companionship, communication, cooperation and the planning of common goals. This is known as *philio* or brotherly and sisterly of love. It is not to be the only form of love within the marital relationship but it is an important form of our intimate bond. Storge, or family love, is generally expressed in our honoring of our parents and our nurture for our children.

AGAPE

Agape is self-giving love, gift love, the love that goes on loving even when the other becomes unlovable. *Agape* love is not just something that happens, it is something you must make happen. Love is a personal act of commitment.

Christ's love (and hence the pattern for our love) is gift love. Christ's love is unconditional. Christ's love is eternal love. *Agape* is kindness. It is being sympathetic, thoughtful, and sensitive to the needs of your loved one. *Agape* is contentment and agape love is a forgiving love.

Individuals who put forth an effort to purposely increase philio and agape love will see all areas of love increase. Friendship love can enhance and enrich both of the others. Agape love in turn can increase and enrich the eros and storge love so that neither diminish. Eros love can flourish if properly nurtured, and if so, the other types of love are reinforced. All four must be given conscious effort.

THE NEED TO DEMONSTRATE LOVE

In any marriage, it is important to demonstrate your love for your spouse. What can you do to demonstrate love?

Your love will either live or die. What kills love? Love dies when you spend little or no time together and when you stop sharing activities that are mutually enjoyable. Love is created or destroyed by pairing or failing to pair the partner with pleasurable activities over a period of time. Love dies from failure on the part of both individuals to reinforce appropriate behavior in each other. Smiling, caressing, complimenting, showing compassion, and spending time together are behaviors in marriage that should be reinforced. If they are not reinforced, they may disappear. If your partner stops doing things that you like, your feelings of love may diminish.

An example of that can be seen in a young couple that I was able to talk to in a large Midwestern church. I had been sharing on the basic concepts or love and the need to keep love alive and they were very curious to explore in greater depth this teaching. As the young couple began to share their story with me it became rather apparent that they had experienced some very difficult expectations, bitterness and hurt together. The young man had been raised in a family where the mother took care of every detail of his life. He had been highly dependent, very happily so, upon his mom and saw the role of his wife as being that of his mother. He wanted the same sense of comfort in being taken care of as his mother had provided. The woman had been raised to be independent; to be self-reliant. This was clearly in conflict with what her husband wanted. Because they had such differing expectations of one another, they began to treat one another with coldness and distance, taking a selfish, defensive position with one another. This was the beginning of their mutual perception that their love and commitment toward one another was waning.

In cases such as this, love must be renewed by conscious change in attitude and behavior towards each other. The necessary change was more difficult for ht self absorbed young man, but in time and with much conscious effort, adjustments were made and love was indeed renewed.

SEX IN MARRIAGE

If large groups of men and women were asked to compare their version of a perfect lover[8] with what they believed to be the version of the opposite sex, many would reply without hesitation that men's and women's images of the ideal lover were worlds apart.

Like most human hostilities, however, "the battle of the sexes" is based on perceived differences that are more imaginary

---

[8] Obviously, within marriage.

than real. The fact is, men and women share remarkable similarities in their tastes in both lovers and love making. Who said what? Two surveys asked large numbers of men and women which personal attributes were most important to them in a lover. Bernie Zilbergeld compiled women's descriptions in his book, <u>*Male Sexuality*</u> and Anthony Pietropinto and Jacqueline Simenauer cataloged men's opinions in <u>*Beyond the Male Myth*</u>. Sample desired attributes from both surveys are listed below. Can you distinguish the traits desired by the men from those desired by the women?

Mature	Sensitive
Honest	A listener
Kind	Fun
Cares	Intelligent
Really listens	Supportive
Good body	Tender
Outgoing	Playful
Intelligent	Sensual
Sense of humor	Enjoys our bodies
Needs me	Sexually communicative
Friendly	Tolerates imperfections
Affectionate	Willing to experiment
Warm	Encouraging
Dresses well	Sharing
Emotional	Caring

Notice how similar the lists are. The column on the left came from the men, the one on the right from the women, but the two can be basically interchanged.

Women often believe that men judge them by their figures, or in the subtle parlance of the men's magazines, by their breasts. It's no coincidence that books on flattening the stomach and enlarging the bust pepper the Best Seller List. A few of the thousands of men Pietropinto and Simenauer surveyed said a woman's figure was a consideration in their selection of lovers, but it was almost always a minor consideration compared to the attributes listed above.

Sex in marriage is supposed to grow and bloom into the best of intimate physical communication. In some marriages, "things" are getting better every day. There are other marriages where sexual expressions (and not just intercourse) have become ruts of routine or non-existent. The Bible talks about the specific purposes for human sexuality, as intended by God, in three primary and integrated ways.

PROCREATION

In read Genesis 1:28 and Deuteronomy 7:13-14, one can see clear evidence that sexual activity for the human race is part of God's design. What is our attitude supposed to be towards human sexuality and human reproduction? God sees sexuality as a positive experience, designed by God for the blessing of man and woman. However, sex was not just for procreation, but also for...

RECREATION AND RELEASE

In Song of Solomon 4:10-12 and Proverbs 5:18-19, you will find, as shocking as it may seem, that the Scriptures actually encourage the enjoyment and the sensual nature of sexual relationships. It seems as though enjoyment of sex is a delightful activity that God has created for all to enjoy within the confines and safety of marriage.

Furthermore, if you look carefully at Proverbs 5:18-19, the writer uses poetic language as he speaks of sexual energies, drive, and outlets. Throughout the Bible favorite symbols for sex include water fountains, streams, cisterns, springs, wells, etc. God made us the way we are, so that we might enjoy one another within the marital union.

COMMUNICATION

In Genesis 2:24 is found the first teaching about the one flesh concept. Beautiful, poetic language presents the coming together or blending together of spirit, mind and soul, the entire being, with ones spouse. There could be no more intimate communication between a husband and wife than through intimate sexual relationships. That may or may not be procreative, but is certainly recreative for both!

HOW DID WE LEARN ABOUT SEX?

(OR, HOW DID SEX GET SO COMPLICATED?)

There are so many misconceptions in the church and the world in general about human sexuality. Even in our age of "sexual revolution", many misconceptions continue. We must remember that most of our basic attitudes, beliefs and feelings expressed about human sexuality were learned within the family, the educational system, church and in some cases, in the back alley or on the playground, depending upon where one was raised.

God places a responsibility upon parents to teach their children the appropriate and proper caring attitudes about sexuality, its proper place within God's plan for mankind, and positive attitudes towards sexual relations within marriage. Unfortunately, few, if any of us, had such training. We hope that the next generation of parents will take seriously the need to train their own children in what God took great care to teach us through His Word.

What are the essential elements of sex education from a Christian perspective? First, to reiterate, parents are responsible for children's sexual behavior. One class member once said that if "sex was mentioned around his parents when he was growing up, his mom would faint and his dad would have a fit." To this day, our mothers tend to be more open about sexuality than our fathers, contrary to popular thought.

Secondly, one element of sex education is to help ensure that a young person is well adjusted sexually, capable of communicating with peers about sexual issues. Further, he hope is that a child will have fully embraced his/her sexual identity as male or female. Most clear research concludes that sexual orientation is determined through multiple factors, including genetics and interrelationships within the family and society in general. There is no conclusive research to indicate that homosexuality is an inbred, genetic trait, though certain characteristics may predispose one towards homosexual tendencies. Though it is not genetic, it is a highly complex issue, and a thorough discussion of human sexuality, its normality's and abnormities, is beyond the scope of this work.

Finally, we need to teach our children the ability to give and receive love. More on this topic will be presented as issues of teen-age dating are discussed, later in the book.

Another important element of sex education is to ensure that our children know who they are in Christ. Every young person needs to know that God has clear expectations for our sexual behavior. We must encourage them to follow biblical norms, these in spite of current beliefs about sexuality. They must be taught the rights as well as the responsibilities of sexual behavior. They need to learn that sexuality is sacred and God given, and worth waiting marriage for.

Sex education includes teaching that sexuality is an extension of our personalities and therefore cannot be excluded from our relationships with other people. The thought that we can have sex with someone without an exchange of self, or of giving away a part of ourselves is a terrible fallacy with dire consequences. When we have sex with someone other than the one God intended us to have sex with, we lose a bit of ourselves in the process.

Healthy sexuality is not instantaneous, but learned. Children are not asexual before puberty, and we shouldn't treat them as though they are. God created us male or female and we need to be treated in such a way to accent the maleness or femaleness, and the specialness of that sex before God and one another.

Another important area of sex education has to do with body sensitivity. Listed here are several areas of body sensitivity that deserve attention.

- Sex cannot be separated from our bodies; it is a part of us.
- We must respect our bodies and the bodies of others.

- Touching is very important to sex education. It is also very important in a marital relationship to learn to touch, care, and caress.
- Body contact means you care for or cherish the person.
- Body contact is a form of security; it gives a sense of warmth and caring.
- Body contact tells a person that they are worthwhile. We all need to have a sense of security and acceptance for who we are as people. We certainly learn that as infants in our initial bond with our mothers via body contact. It is a God given need that we will always have.
- Body contact shows possession. When we have close intimate body contact with another human being, there is a form of transference of self and possession that occurs. That is why we need to be so careful with whom we share our bodies.

It is important to remember that we can teach intimacy by first living an intimate life before our children. Do not be afraid to show affection to one another. I still remember seeing my mother and father hug and kiss, even occasionally pat each other in places of importance. As kids we would giggle and yet we recognized the love and caring that they had each for other. Kids need to know that mom and dad love each other and parents can help lay groundwork for healthy future expectations by demonstrating open affection.

Make It Easy

Make a child feel comfortable when they ask questions about sex. Do not look shocked, do not run away, do not refer them to the father/mother, but be willing to answer questions openly and frankly with the children. Whatever you do, do not lie to them. Recognize that if you tell them the actual parts of the anatomy and how the sexual act occurs, as a young child, they are probably not going to understand it fully, but it will not warp them. In fact, they will find out later that mom and dad were straight and told them the truth. They will respect that!

In some cases, where there are sexual problems, counseling may be necessary. Do not be ashamed, especially if there is a child of pre-pubescent age that is overly preoccupied with sex, or it seems as though that they have no interest in the opposite sex in the teen-age years. Sometimes it is helpful to seek special expertise outside of the family.

Much can be learned about our reproductive system from good books. It is also important that we build self-esteem in ourselves and take pride in the way we are. We cannot divorce ourselves from our sexual feelings, but must integrate them into the broader themes of fidelity and love.

"Unless we gratify our sex desire, the race is last; unless we restrain it, we destroy ourselves."
Bernard Shaw

PROBLEMS IN MARRIAGE AND HOW TO SOLVE THEM

Roles, Responsibilities And Decision Making

There are so many problems that can crop up in a modern

day marriage. The stress on marriage is tremendous and problems will occur partially because of those stresses, partially because we are incomplete human beings, and partially because Satan is truly like a roaring lion seeking to devour individuals, and to destroy families from within. One of the most difficult areas in family life has to do with the issues raised by the roles or responsibilities of family life and who makes decisions within the family unit.

What are the questions of roles and responsibilities in marriage? Who does what, and why does he/she do it? Is it because of tradition, because of what the church has said, or is it because it is the way it was done in the family of origin?

Failure to clarify husband/wife roles in a relationship is a major cause of marital disruption. Daily, couples involve themselves in an almost endless number of activities and responsibilities. Each couple should discuss and decide who is most competent to do each task. Assignment of a task should not be made simply because of parental example, nor because it is expected in a social group, or because of tradition. When an individual's ability, training, and temperament make it difficult or unnecessary to follow an established cultural norm for a role, the couple will need to have the strength to establish their own style of working together. It is imperative that a couple **deliberately and mutually** develop the rules and guidelines for their relationship as husband and wife. This clear assignment of authority and responsibility between the spouses does not create a rigid relationship but allows flexibility and order in what could become a chaotic mess.

A WOMAN'S PLACE: WHERE ARE YOU?

Misconceptions of a woman's role can cause great conflict as does the often misunderstood issue of submission of women within the local church. Briefly discussed below are beliefs that many hold regarding the place of women.

The first is the belief that women are "property," that is, that the wife has almost no rights and privileges compared to those of the husband. The husband is the family provider. Often the wife is perceived as merely chattel for the husband's sexual expression.

The second is to perceive the woman's' role as complementary. This belief allows for an increase in the wife's rights and privileges. Marriage remains the wife's central life interest. The husband is chief provider and has more authority or power than the wife. She is a friend to her husband. He achieves and she supports him. Primary conflicts may occur if the wife attempts to expand her role, or if the husband feels she is not adequately supporting him.

The third concept is the wife as a "junior partner". In this marital model the wife's rights increase because she works outside the home for pay. Her main motive is to improve the family's life style. She has more authority (rights) than a nonworking woman. Conflicts over time, household responsibilities, male ego infringement (if she makes more money), and fatigue can be prevalent.

The last concept is that of "equal partners". As equal partners, the husband and wife share equal rights and responsibilities. This is the spiritual ideal as indicated in

Ephesians 5:21. Roles and responsibilities are negotiated between partners. Husbands seek to love their spouses sacrificially and wives respect their husbands for the responsible position they have under Christ's headship. The relationship is not competitive but rather complementary. This is an ideal we must strive for and can obtain with God's grace.

SUBMISSION

Submission has been taken out of its Biblical context by many persons in the Fundamentalist/Charismatic community. The strong teaching in fundamentalist circles on headship and submission may seem spiritual (or convenient), but it is theologically - biblically naive. Far too many Christians let others do their thinking for them, rather than conducting a thorough study of God's word on a matter.

Servants of the Lord are not "favored" positionally in the Word of God. "Elitism" does not co-exist with servanthood. Headship involves servanthood, life-giving, and facilitation of others. Biblical Christianity does not foster "male Elitism" in the name of submission.

Leaders (heads) are not above responsible counsel. It is self-serving to hide behind "we should not criticize." Counsel is beneficial when it drives one to the truth in the area of relationships. We are being duped or "dumped on" by some denominational/institutional leaders, Christian "celebrities", and some pastors who try to hide mistakes and fear behind the facade of false spirituality.

Let me give you some examples of the poor use of the concept of submission: First, some commend Sarah for lying. She "obeyed" her husband as was her "duty." Is this a good example to follow? What about a wife sleeping with a business associate to furthermore her husband's career, because she "should obey" her husband?

Second, breaking a child's spirit....even if he dies! There have been sad cases where a wife remained quiet while her husband abused their child. She said it was not her place to usurp her husband's authority. She was taught that a woman cannot override her husband's authority by promulgators of "Christian submission" in a seminar, giving her "permission" to neglect her logical duties to protect her child.

Third, is Sapphira good example? She didn't interfere with her husband's ploy either, as seen in Acts, Chapter 5. Obviously, she suffered the consequences of her decision, right along with her husband. It is so important that we develop a balanced view on this topic.

Are women to obey God or their husbands in moral/ethical spheres? Is the universal priesthood of believers with direct access to God through the efficacy of Christ's blood valid? We are all equal in Christ, in fact, our goal is mutual submission one to another, loving one another as servant/leaders, not taking a role above someone else because we believe that we deserve it or because we have been born a certain gender.

HEADERSHIP

One area of the submission conflict is seen in the concept of headship. What is headship, and how is it explained within the Word of God?

There are only two places where a man or husband is referred to as "head" (I Corinthians 11:1-16 and Ephesians 5:21-23). In the I Corinthians passage, headship carries the notation of "being the source of life and existence." Nowhere in the context is there a discussion of an authoritarian ruling over the wife by the husband. In Ephesians 5, Paul begins with an old concept familiar to the people to whom he is speaking, but then he fills it with new meaning and expands its emphasis towards the oneness which God initially intended for marriage. The emphasis on headship is no longer to be a matter of rank or power. Headship is to take on a new meaning, not only as superior leader, but also self-giving servant.

Furthermore, Paul used the example of Christ's self-sacrificing action on behalf of the church. This example alone defines the meaning of headship. As Christ gave himself in love and humbled himself, so husbands are to take the initiative in building an atmosphere of loving, self-sacrificing service. The clear picture is one of love and service. Headship/leadership in the home may be more clearly seen as a facilitating activity. In short, headship/leadership becomes a matter of performing certain functions that move or facilitate a group, organization, or family toward its goals. The concept of the body or the church being composed of many parts, each fulfilling a unique function and purpose, seems to apply in this context. Headship/leadership is seen as accepting responsibility and performing certain functions. In the marital relationship, headship/leadership should be practiced in such a way that it advances both members toward the goal of oneness.

Nothing by way of statement or through the model of

Christ's action conveys the idea that one partner is made more responsible for the actions of the church. As is said in Galatians 3:28,

> "There is neither Jew or Greek, slave or free,
> male or female, for all are one in Christ Jesus."

Members of the body of Christ are individually responsible and accountable to God for their own actions,

> "The (father)....shall be put to death for his own
> sin." (Deuteronomy 24:16)

Though functions will differ depending upon gifts and abilities, each individual in the marriage are equal partners in a journey to fulfill godly purposes through their marriage.

Headship/leadership presupposes a self-sacrificing love, which directs the husband to take an active involvement in facilitating and encouraging his wife. He also encourages his marriage toward the ultimate pattern of oneness without being threatened when his wife, who is equally involved, grows and develops. Just as Christ creates conditions whereby the church may become whole, so the husband will create conditions and opportunities for the wife to move toward maturity and fulfillment as a person.
Furthermore, the wife is to show proper respect (the foundation upon which love is built) to her husband in private and public. This respect is not based upon the husband's ability but his position as determined by God in His Word.

GUIDELINES FOR TODAY

The Christian community should provide the best environment for dealing with the concerns of marriage, divorce, remarriage, and human sexuality. The church knows the One who is able to transform all human life, and as a redeemed fellowship has the capacity to reach those afflicted by loneliness, divorce, or marital discord. It realizes their true potential is in Christ. It can also provide for its members a distinctive foundation for marriage in God's Word. Where the members are concerned for and accountable to each other, there will be concern for each marriage, each divorce, and each remarriage because the church is aware of its impact on the children, on their common life, and on the church's witness in the world. In each case, the church can acknowledge Christ as Redeemer and Lord.

FORGIVENESS

Marital disruption is one of the most severe tests of the Christian concept of grace. The church is called to be a fellowship where those who falter and fail can rebuild their lives and where the divorced can find love and patient support. Some congregations (including elders and ministers) have not developed their ability to exercise the forgiveness of Christ toward repentant adulterers and divorcees. Yet the Bible indicates that failures or sins in these areas are no more grievous than other sins, nor any less forgivable. Paul rightly admonishes, "Let grace abound," not that there might be more sin, but that there may be new life (Rom. 5:20-6:2). Christian realism includes acknowledging the new possibilities included in God's forgiveness. Where the one flesh relationship has been irreconcilably shattered, divorce may occur. In fact, where a marriage has been destroyed, especially through abuse, neglect or unrepented infidelity, the Christian community may counsel severance to prevent further damage to persons involved. Likewise, in counseling divorced persons considering remarriage, a minister is often compelled to decide which is the better of two difficult alternatives. Each case must be examined on its own merits. Whether the minister should agree to officiate a remarriage or not, he should share his reasons with the couple. The Word and Spirit, the mind of the Church, and one's own conscience must be considered in making the decision.

Those who have undergone the trauma of divorce need time to reflect upon their experience and time to rebuild. First, persons should take time for reflection on the causes of the previous failure. Repentance is necessary. It involves not only penitence for one's own part, but a change in one's attitude and actions. Harmful personality traits and behavioral patterns must be transformed before remarriage is considered. Second, personal realization of God's forgiveness is a vital part of one's readiness for remarriage. This includes forgiving the former partner and seeking forgiveness. Otherwise a residue of bitterness can cloud future interpersonal relations. Continuing obligations to the former mate or children, financial and otherwise, should be met. Third, there must be a vision of what the new marriage can mean and the determination to make it Christ centered. Recognition of human limitations at this point rightly leads one to a reliance on Christ and on the supportive family of faith. Willingness to be a full participant with the people of God is prerequisite to proceeding with remarriage. Where the forgiveness of God has been accepted and life redirected to obedient service, the prospects for a sound marriage exist.

GROWTH

Growth within a marriage relationship is vital if joy and gratitude for God's gift are to continue. Where only individual development, personal pleasure, and professional advancement are stressed, the result is generally a moving apart. Such priorities dominate many social circles with corrosive effect. In contrast, the church offers three goals which call for mutual growth and service. First, marriage as designed by God calls for couples to strive for a heightened sensitivity to each other and a deepening relationship in the Spirit. Second, God intends that each may uphold and complement the other over the years that there may be mutual fulfillment. Finally, God desires that couples guide their children in the Christian life, and that they, as a family, be Christ's witnesses in their community.

CONCLUSION

Marriage remains a beautiful but fragile gift because, like the gospel, "we have this treasure in earthen vessels." Nevertheless, we rejoice in this gift because God's transcendent power works in and through it (II Cor. 4:7). Therefore, in marriage our goal is always that "the life of Jesus may be manifested in our mortal flesh" (II Cor. 4:11). Now we will begin to turn our intention to the next stage of the family life cycle; the development of the family.

SECTION II

FAMILY

"The family you come from isn't as important as the family you're going to have."
Ring Lardner

SECTION II

THE FAMILY

As with marriage, which originates with God, we must look at the family from God's original perspective. What was/is God's plan for the family?

TO BUILD A HOUSE

In Psalms 127:1, the word states that
"Unless the Lord builds the house, they labor in vain who build it."

The first institution that God created (beginning with marriage) is the family. When God spoke, he created order out of chaos. It is still his plan, within the family unit (and the church, the family of God) to create a living organism which is able to reflect the creative and redemptive nature and purpose of God.

As noted in the previous section, marriage begins the process of developing a full and rich family life. It starts with a leaving and cleaving, and leads to a "knowing" (sexual intimacy) which usually leads to the production of children. This is the ultimate expression of mutual love for the mature couple.

FAMILY LIFE

The Bible does not outline a division of labor for the family. The specific details or individual dance steps of a couple or family are usually worked out through trial and error, conflict and compromise. Much of the "how" of married life, child rearing, financial management, priorities and goals, are predetermined prior to matrimony. That is, all couples bring into family life preconceived beliefs, attitudes and desires that will naturally differ from one another. Thus, a mature couple will recognize early on that there are few right and wrong ways to accomplish tasks. The goal is a loving agreement between the couple, unity of mind and purpose based upon time, talent and desire.

TIME

As family life progresses, time becomes a precious commodity. Between work, chores, cooking, cleaning, soccer and dance lessons, modern families are exceedingly engaged. Thus, time and is usage becomes important. Often, who does what in terms of tasks (such as chores) depends more on who has the time than anything else. Frankly, it seems to be a reason to have lots of children, to have someone to do the chores!

TALENT

Talent can also determine who does what. As a child, I learned to clean the kitchen and bath, and have never minded the work. Being good at the task, I am happy to take responsibility to see them accomplished. However, having never mastered the basics of carpentry or auto mechanics (stereotypical male duties), I am happy to delegate or hire these tasks out whenever possible.

DESIRE

Finally, desire can play a part. If one spouse has a neat fetish, than by all means they should exercise their compulsion by taking on the tidiness task. Things people like to do always become easier to manage; doing things you enjoy makes any job, even housework smoother.

FOUNDATIONS

In spite of the lack of Biblical specifics, there are some overriding principles of healthy family living that lays a foundation to build a house upon. They can be seen as family activities that are common (though not always evident at the time), in healthy, functional families. These are worth noting and studying.

LOVE

Many would think that love in the family should be a given. However, Paul the apostle instructs men in no uncertain terms of their duty to love (agape) their wives as Christ does His church. (Eph. 6) Furthermore, the elder women were admonished and encouraged to teach younger women to love their husbands and children. (Titus 2:4-8) They were to be an example and provide wise counsel to those who lacked "natural" love in their home. With the high incidence of spousal and child abuse, family abandonment and divorce, this is a skill that needs to be taught for the preservation and growth of our families.

UNITY

In Matthew 19:4-6, Jesus reiterates the Genesis account of marriage. Christ emphasizes the "one flesh" relationship, where individual goals and needs become secondary to the familial responsibilities. The highest form of this, and certainly the heart beat of Jesus (see John 17) is unity. After this is unity in diversity. That is, though there are many wonderful and unique differences between men, women and children, with God's help these differences can be blended into a unified team that can fulfill God's purpose and the family's destiny.

PEACE

It has been stated that the home is a man's castle. It is a safe place, separate from the world and its pressures. This of course is the ideal scenario. Very few homes reflect the TV image of old, (The Nelson's, The Cleaver's, The Brady's, or The Walton's) but are often more like modern sitcoms. In truth, God has called the family to be a haven of rest. (Eph. 6:1-4). A well ordered house filled with God's love and love for one another, where unity is exhibited without compromise, can be and frequently is a place of peace.

TRAINING AND TEACHING

The home is to be the primary place of instruction for children. Prov. 22:1-6, speaks of righteous training (to guide, direct, correct, encourage) of children by both mom and dad. Though salvation is not promised, habitual patterns that we build into our children will become manifest (whether good or bad) when they reach their majority.

Along with training comes teaching, which is also a family activity. Where as traditionally (and in most homes, practically), the mother is the primary trainer, it is the father who is seen as primarily responsible for instruction. Children need to be taught the principles of fairness, justice, mercy and wisdom, as well as skills for eventual independent/interdependent living. The task of training and teaching (and of learning), is a life long process to be valued within the home.

WORSHIP

In the plan of God, worship of the Lord is a family affair. When the day of Pentecost arrived and the church was birthed, from that day, it met for fellowship, prayer, teaching, and communion in homes. (Acts 2:42) Furthermore, worship was a normal part of the faithful's home. (see Acts 10:1-4). Whether formal or informal, daily or periodically, an emphasis on worshipping the Lord in the family is vital. Since strong families make strong churches and communities, anything we do to strengthen the home should be supported. Worship, in all of its forms, in the home goes a long way towards accomplishing this godly priority.

A REMINDER

Rome was not built in a day, nor will a family or house be built to the glory of God in a few weeks or months. It takes years of patience and endurance through life's ups and downs to produce a family that is able to stand the test of time. Developing ones family life on a sure, Biblical foundation is a first and crucial step to ensuring a house of honor for the Lord.

CHANGES IN FAMILIES

Over the last forty to fifty years there have been significant changes within Western family systems that have affected us all. These changes have been tremendous, and in many cases traumatic. In this brief section we are going to look at some of the changes that have occurred and how they have affected the Western family.[9]

Families have moved from rural areas to urban. As is well documented, the needs in urban centers of the United States and around the world are great. One main emphasis in world missions is to reach these urban centers with the gospel. Cities are crying out for hope from God. In these urban centers is readily seen breakdown within the family due to poverty, racism, and the other forces of evil that come against individuals and families.

Furthermore, families have moved from being production to consumption oriented. Psychologically we would say that much of America is a "me oriented" society; the consumption of goods that will please the senses and make one happy has become a chief obsession. Historically, the West has lived according to a protestant work ethic, essentially stating that "we must work, striving to do things for the good of the whole." Unfortunately, the work ethic has deteriorated significantly over the past decades, although there are some signs of a rebound in the 21st century.

Families have shifted from an economy of scarcity to an economy of abundance. We live in a society that has more of an abundance of products, more wealth than at any other time in the history of the world. Yet, in the midst of great wealth there remains poverty and significant need. Though families tend to work less and have more recreation time, one of the primary problems seen in the

---

[9] With notable exceptions (fundamentalist Muslim, strict Buddhist, etc.) the West has , for good or ill, affected the cultures of most nations. Assuming nations will eventually be judged by God, The West will have much to answer for in regards to our many unhealthy exports.

counseling office evolves from the anxiety experienced due in part to the inability to deal with this new found freedom. It has lead many to obsessive materialism as an attempt to fulfill a real or perceived need.

Also, families have had to learn to cope with the higher cost cost of living. The ravages of inflation have affected most families within Western culture, as in the rest of the world. It even affects members of the church, especially as we compare our lives to overbearing preachers. Many people say, "Where is the prosperity for me?" Inflation, poverty, and other problems can be devastating for the common family.

Furthermore, families have more complex and flexible rules to live by. Before the turn of the century, the rules by which people operated, the way relationships worked, seemed clear and understandable. Today, especially with the sexual revolution and the upheaval of the sixties, seventies, and eighties has caused great confusion for many. Because of this, families have an increasing amount of instability in the way they function. The roles and responsibilities of family members can become blurred. This strengthens the need for the gospel message, and living a Christian family life. There is a need for renewed stability, which can only be founded upon a clear understanding and appropriation of the Word of God.

COMPARISONS ABOUND

How does the traditional family compare with the contemporary family? A simple comparison of contemporary/traditional family systems will suffice. The traditional family begins with patriarchal rule, whereas the contemporary family, at least on the surface, is more equalitarian, or democratic. The traditional family functions as an interdependent unit. This is contrasted with the more contemporary style, which includes employment outside of the home by one or two family members, necessitating greater independence. Traditional families were religiously committed, whereas modern families are largely secular with church taking a secondary role. Traditional families practiced unrestricted childbearing, the more children the better. Today, Planned Parenthood reigns supreme. For many a couple, to have more than two or three children is seen as almost sinful, even amongst Christian's.

Traditional family's leisure time was limited to and centered on the home. Contemporary society's leisure time is expanded in scope and much time is spent on commercialized activities. As a result of this, families do not know how to play together. This is especially seen in dysfunctional family systems where the ability to laugh is limited and uncommon, and many are unable to share love in an open and caring way. Traditional family structure believed that mate selection was a family concern and parents exerted great influence in marital choices. Today, mate selection is an individualistic matter based, often times, upon biochemistry with the parents playing a much smaller or insignificant role. The heart frequently overrules the head.

Education of the family was a family responsibility. In a traditional family much of the education was done at home or in small family units. Today our educational system is relegated to non-family social agencies, both public and private, although that has changed some with the relatively recent wave of home schooling. Traditional families have moved from stable and rigid social and moral value positions to relatively unstable and diversified value structures of contemporary society. In traditional families the role of the wife was homemaker, housekeeper, and mother; the role of the father was provider and protector. Today the wife is just as frequently working outside of the home and in many cases is more involved in community activities and leadership. Subsequently the father is more actively involved in the care of children and the upkeep of the family structure.

How have these things changed the Christian family? Many people would say that the changes have been for the better, some for the worse. My sense is that the changes are just that, they are changes. Change is frightening for many people and as Christians we must be willing to make adjustments to fit contemporary society without compromising our Christian values. This is often a difficult task for families to accomplish. Thus, the need for church and church leaders to be PG-rated (parental guidance) is strongly suggested!

THE MOMENTOUS CHANGE

Around the world, men and woman will make a life-changing step this year. Not only will this step change their lives, it will have a profound effect on the next generation as well.

THEY WILL HAVE CHILDREN

How they raise these youngsters will have a greater impact on society than the way they vote, the art they create, the book they read, the technological problems they solve, or the planets they visit in space. And yet, perhaps never before in the world's history have parents faced and felt more pressure or sought more professional help in the rearing of their children.

As can be seen from the family life developmental process, there are many major transitions that occur within a couple's life. The first one being courtship, then marriage. The next major transitional comes when a couple decides to have children. In this section we are going to discuss some of the practical problems which may develop as a young couple become parents (for an extensive study on Parenting, see the author's book, *Parenting On Purpose.*

As you read, you may want to explore your own feelings, perceptions, and belief systems in regards to parenting and your relationship to your spouse in regards to children.

What are some of the practical problems which may develop in parenthood? First of all, a couple may not want children at all. Or, one of the members of the marriage may want children and the other may not. This can cause tremendous stress on a marriage relationship and should be thoroughly discussed and agreed to before a couple marries. Unfortunately, this does not occur in all cases and may cause a schism in the marital relationship.

Secondly, school or employment needs of the adults may conflict with family plans. Again, as mentioned many times, couples come into a relationship with certain perceptions and beliefs about what should and shouldn't be a part of that relationship. These too should be discussed before children are considered.

Third, a couple may not be able to have children for a physical reason and may need to consider adoption. This is not necessarily a tragic situation, but certainly one that a couple would have to deal with together and with support and sensitivity of friends, the family and the church.

Fourthly, very few couples prepare themselves psychologically for having children. Children take time and care. A mature couple recognizes this and is able to make necessary adjustments in their lifestyle to accommodate this radical change. Where a couple is immature, or one still has expectations that their spouse should give them the sole attention in the family, there can be significant problems. A couple needs to become psychologically prepared for having children. This can come through several formats, such as church teaching, couples classes, retreats or mentoring.

Another possible problem that may develop in parenthood is the determination of the number of children a couple will have and how far apart in age they should be. There is no hard and fast rule as to what is the best form of spacing...I've seen very happy families where the spacing is four or five years apart and others where they are nine to ten months apart. Each has their own set of possibilities and problems which need to be talked through between the husband and wife.

Another concern for couples is the actual process or period of pregnancy. Pregnancy itself, we must remember, is not an illness. The having of children is a blessing of God. But the process can be difficult for many couples, with such wonderful gifts as morning sickness, the possibility of miscarriages, the changes in sexual desires one for another, even the sense of loss of self-esteem that the wife may experience because she begins to "blossom" physically.

Much insecurity within the relationship can become evident during pregnancy. Certain allowances must be made for the wife, because she is not able to take care of all of the heavy tasks that she could have before. A sensitive husband is one that is able to understand his spouse's special needs and lend the extra helping hand as necessary.

Provisions must be made for the adequate care in nurturing of a new child, both physically and emotionally. These provisions should be thought through in advance. The Bible says that we need to count the cost before any endeavor. This is especially true before bringing children into the world. However, if we wait until we can "fully afford" children, we may never get around to having them. However, adjustments certainly need to be prayerfully considered and judicially made.

SHIFTING ROLES

There are many new roles for both father and mother. Up until the conception and birth of a child a couple is primarily focused on taking care of and nurturing one another. Now "baby making three" brings a whole new set of roles and expectations. We are now parents..., we are mom and dad! Unfortunately, most of us automatically "buy into" the role of mother and father as we learned it from our family of origin. It is vitally important that husbands and wives clearly communicate with one another what their needs and expectations are. Who does the 2 o'clock feedings? Does dad do diapers? Is it only the mother's role to take care of the child while the father continues to do what he was doing...only playing with the child when he comes home at night? These are all things that should be fully discussed, and agreements need to be made (preferably in writing and best with a mature witness!).

There is also the need for the reallocating of income to meet the new financial needs. The couple that may be used to going out to dinner once or twice a week may not be able to continue their lifestyle when children come home.

Furthermore, positive communication with relatives and friends and between husband and wife must be developed. Physical and emotional needs begin to change when children arrive. It is not unusual for one or the other of the parents to feel neglected or left out of the life of their spouse. At times they may feel jealously towards the new addition to the home. As much of a joy that children can be, they can also be a painful experience. They are inconvenient, they cry at all the wrong times, and they contribute nothing to the maintenance of the status quo.

Therefore, there is a need for the sharing of time and affection with the children. The couple must not neglect the husband and wife's need for affection and time. It is important to take time for one's spouse to renew and strengthen their relationship on a regular basis.

Most young couples can significantly benefit from education in child rearing that includes spiritual training, purposeful parenting, and all phases of child development.[10] If the husband and wife disagree about the raising and training of the children and what values they

---

[10] For an excellent study on stages of development, see Dr. Bohac's book, *"Human Development: A Christian Perspective*

wish them to espouse, serious problems can occur. An example of that could be seen in the socialization of a typical boy in almost any culture. Many times they are allowed to present certain types of behaviors that girls are not. Fathers (especially) may wink at disobedient behavior because it reminds them a bit of their own mischievousness as a child. It is important for parents to look beyond themselves and their personal needs, focusing instead on the needs of their children, regardless of how difficult a task this may seem to be.

The focus of parenting is the positive shaping of a child's behavior to love God and their neighbor as themselves.

Remember, children need discipline, which includes care, nurturing and at times punishment. In fact, there are three primary components necessary for children to grow to maturity. First, children need a limited amount of freedom. Children need to have opportunity to explore their environment, even to make mistakes. That is one way that they develop of confidence and curiosity, which is the way God made us.

Secondly, children need discipline; both teaching and correction. Children need to know their limits. Later in the book you will see practical guidelines regarding appropriate child discipline based upon the age and needs of children. But, thirdly, children need unconditional love. The famous psychotherapist Carl Rogers coined the phrase unconditional positive regard. He turned this concept into a counseling technique whereby a counselor will listen attentively and give total positive caring towards another person without judgment, regardless of the problems that they might have. Certainly, that is the way God treats us, with unconditional love *"in that while we were yet sinners, Christ died for us"* (Romans 5:8).

Yet any of these three areas, if provided to a child out of balance, can cause damage to the child's growth and development. Too much freedom and a child learns that he/she has no limits and is likely to develop a disregard for authority later in life. One who is too coercively disciplined may be prone to depression, anxiety and develop fears regarding facing the world. Total unconditional love without discipline and freedom is mere sentimentality and gives the child a sense of omnipotence rather than learning to conform to basic rules. It is important to have all three key elements in proper balance. Of course, no one can or will do this perfectly. We can only do our best and let God take care of the rest.

Finally, parents need to be positive role models for their children. We should be a positive parental example in the way we live and converse, because just as you learned from your parents by what they did more than by what they said, so will your children learn from you.

PRACTICAL PRINCIPLES IN CHRISTIAN PARENTHOOD

What are some practical principles for couples to apply in Christian parenthood? A review will help. First and foremost, it is essential for a Christian parent to seek the Lord's will and direction in family planning. This happens through prayer, through study of the Word, and through seeking wise counsel. Whether that be from a pastor, a professional marriage & family therapist, social worker, or Christian psychologist, it is important to seek the Lord's will and direction.

Secondly, we must remember that children are gifts from the Lord and it is our privilege to have them (Psalm 127:3-5). Every parent, at times, wishes they could somehow send their children back where they came, but there is no such thing as a return to sender policy when it comes to children. They are truly a gift and a challenge. It is also important to consider the number of children and the spacing of children, even during the engagement period, or, at least, in the very early part of the marriage. Couples must realistically face the economic and parental responsibility of having children. It would be irresponsible to have more children than what one can financially afford to take care for.

Furthermore, a couple must be ready to assume new roles as husband and wife. As stated previously, there are tremendous stresses placed upon the family when a baby comes into the home. Parents can get tired and cranky. We can look at our husband or wife and blame them for not doing as much as perhaps we think they should. Children have a wonderful ability to divide and conquer their parents. Thus, it is very important that both parents communicate well and accept their new roles as something given to them by the Lord.

Be ready to adjust to new time schedules. At the same time don't neglect each other as husband and wife because of new involvements. It is important to stay close to one another and renew the marital covenant often.

Accept the parental responsibility to rear one's children to be good citizens. Parents need to teach children self-control, to come to know the Lord and grow up in Him at an early age. This is an essential part in daily family living.

It is one of our primary responsibilities as Christian parents to raise our children in the nurture and admonition of the Lord. (Eph. 6:4)

Parents need to become, if they are not already, healthy role models in order to develop healthy children. Healthy principles must be practiced by both parents. It is not enough for one of the parents to be a good example while the other lives selfishly. If you are in a family situation where one of the spouses is saved and one is not, God gives special grace to help you to make up the possible negative qualities within your spouse, or at least the less-Christian behavior that they may exhibit.

Be ready to adjust the budget if necessary, and make sure that you have adequate financial provisions. It is important to listen to the counsel of parents, relatives, and friends, but remember that you must live your own lives as a family. Ultimately, God will hold you responsible for how you raise your children. Accept what counsel you can and be appreciative of it.

A SIMPLE EXAMPLE

I remember when my Karen and I had our first child, Rebecca. My mother was able to help my wife care for Rebecca during those difficult first few days. She gave some helpful advice and help, which was a wonderful blessing. On the birth of our second child, Rachel, Karen's mother was able to do much the same. That early advice and help was vital, but later advice was not appropriate and helpful when the discipline of our children was discussed. Both Karen's mom and mine had a very different view of discipline than we did. We were fully convinced of the appropriateness of our view, and were equally committed to disciplining differently our parents had disciplined us. Although we listened graciously to their opinions and advice on discipline issues, we were obligated to agreeably disagree, and insist that discipline be done the way we felt best as God gave wisdom, even if (as it was) contrary our parents previous ways. Remember that you will have good and bad days in rearing a family. You will make mistakes, and become much wiser because of the experience.

Finally, depend unceasingly on the Lord as you enter Christian parenthood. You cannot do the task alone, but the Holy Spirit is ready to help and guide you in the process.

TOOLS FOR CHILD TRAINING

When a child is old enough, encourage the child to dedicate his/her life to the Lord for whatever His will is. One positive aspect of Jewish tradition, sometimes found in historical/liturgical churches, is bar mitzvah or a time of dedication or confirmation for children.

During this special service, occurring at age 12-13, a child is "tested" to ensure their knowledge of God's word, and the child's new status in the family and community. As modeled in the life of Christ (see Luke 2), the child is required to recite scripture, state prayers, etc., and emerges fro the service as a boy/girl (young man/young woman) rather than a child as previous. When done well in conjunction with local church leadership, this "blessing" service can make a powerful impact on the young person. Youth often rise to our expectations, and if we expect maturity, and include them as emerging adults, we often receive our faith filled expectations. Further, this service provides for a natural time to allow the child to make a specific dedication to the Lord of their life, if they have not already done so.

It is important that we treat each child as an individual, knowing his/ her needs and finding ways to meet those needs. Each child is a bit different and has different requirements. Parents must learn to listen to children, to learn of their unique needs. A key to the learning process is to give opportunity for questions within their natural setting. One of the favorite times in our family came when taking a drive, walk, or just going to the store together. These times were used to talk about the simple and the complex, even the things of God. It is amazing what wonderful, sometimes difficult and even significant theological questions that my children presented to me. It was always a challenge to answer them to the best of my ability. Of course, it is important that we avoid preaching at our children. We need to take advantage of every opportunity to use the Word of God to teach proper values, but we need not stuff it down our children's throat.

Husband's and wives' are to work together as well as individually to train their children. This will help a child see the differences between a Christian home from the homes of unsaved friends (hopefully there will be differences). This will also expose him/her to other Christian families so that they can sense the larger picture and importance of membership in the body of Christ. Also, parents are to discipline according to Biblical standards and principles, not according to standards, or lack thereof, presented in the society at large. Furthermore, we need to have clear agreements between husband and wife on spiritual matters; how we are going to treat the children, whether we are going to have family devotions or not, and how they are going to be done, etc.

Teaching the child about God's ownership of his/her body and the need for taking care of it is important as well. Most parents today are well aware of the issues, problems and the tragedy of child abuse. As unfortunate as it is, we need to make our children aware that their body is theirs, given to them by God and not to be used or abused by others. Thus, it helps to create an atmosphere whereby children can ask questions, willing to share if someone does something inappropriate to them. As finances and opportunity allow, parents need to provide good literature, music, and other material to expose the child to teachings that enrich him/her spiritually.

Make tools available for Bible study which should include a study Bible, a concordance, and a commentary for your children. Give them opportunities to allow their natural curiosity about the things of God to be tested and tried as they read the Word. Set goals for your child to see how far he/she is progressing. Children seem to do very well when they work towards something important. If your church does not provide for that, set up in your home times where the children read, perhaps, certain chapters of the Bible and answer certain questions. This will keep them growing in the Lord.

Along with God's word, we need to teach respect and responsibility. The best way to do this is by being respectful and responsible to one another as husband and wife. Do not be guilty of being too busy to care for your family. Sometimes that can be difficult to do in our busy work-a-day world. If necessary, take time management courses, talk to a counselor, or to someone else that you trust and whose time seems to be well organized. Perhaps they can help you to learn to balance your time so you can provide positive care for your family.

Spend time with him/her so they know that you are interested in them and in their spiritual growth. Remember, it takes time to train, especially children. It takes time and energy, but the results are wonderful.

PRAYER IS KEY

It is important to pray for your children, that they will come to know Christ early in life, and that you will train and nurture them in their relationship with God. I came to know Christ as my Savior at the age of 12, shortly after the death of U.S President John F. Kennedy. Up until that time, my parents had faithfully sent my sister, my brother, and I to church. We learned about Jesus, while our parents stayed home Sunday after Sunday. The crisis of John Kennedy's untimely death shook my parents, and they began to attend church. Eventually, because of the faithfulness of many people within that local church, we all came to know Christ as personal Savior and Lord. It took a crisis for our family to come to Christ. I thank God we did. How much better to nurture our children to know Christ from their earliest days and to grow in His love in a family committed to Jesus.

THE ROLES OF CHILDREN

The Scriptures say a great deal about children in the Christian home. The key scriptures are briefly reviewed here. Remember, God has graciously given us children (Genesis 33:5). Children are to obey and honor their parents (Exodus 20:12, Deut. 5:16). Speaking of honoring, that commandment never ends. We are always to respect our parents for who they are. As adults, that doesn't mean we have to do what they say, but we still show them respect for the position that God has placed them in.

Further, children are to learn to obey the voice of the Lord and do what He commands (Deut. 30:2). Children are gifts from the Lord (Psalm 127:3). The book of Proverbs teaches *"A wise son makes a father glad"* (Pro. 10:1, 15:20, 27:11). Children are to listen and pay attention to their father, and not reject their mother when she is old (Pro. 23:22). Children are to respect the Lord (Pro. 24:21). Children learn to fear or respect the Lord primarily by learning to fear their parents, not a fear or dread as though they are going to be wiped off the face of the earth. It is awe and respect that children need to have for parents, which is produced through clear and consistent discipline - setting limits, following through. As children learn to respect their parents, they will also learn a fear for the Lord.

Children are to keep the law. Children are not to rob their parents (Pro. 28:7, 24). In the New Testament, there are also many statements regarding children. First, the Lord Jesus emphasized the importance of little children in his ministry. We are also to have the same concern for our children, and for the children of others (Matt. 19:14, Mark 10:14, Luke 18:16). Children are unstable and unsettled, but we have a responsibility to bring them from where they are to where they ought to be (Eph. 4:14). In Ephesians 6:1 we see that children are to obey their parents, for this is the right thing to do in the sight of God.

WHOSE WHO?

Children are to be in subjection to their parents and they are NOT to rule their house (1 Tim. 3:4). In counseling practice one major problem often discussed is out of control children and teenagers - they are essentially usurping the authority of parents. Neither children nor teenagers are to rule the house. Parents need to recognize that they have a fiduciary responsibility to keep their out of control children in control. This may be difficult at times, and parents may need special help accomplishing this task.

Youth are to be examples of believers in every way. Their youth is not to be despised (1 Tim. 4:12). Young people are to establish a pattern of good works (Titus 2:6-8). Children are to be corrected by their fathers (Hebrews 12:9).

There are many other Scriptures related to children. In fact, if raised in a home that espouses Christian values, children have the opportunity to grow into maturity, becoming examples of good behavior, which will no doubt bring appropriate pride and joy to their parents. Remember of course, there is no such thing as perfect children or perfect parents. If they existed, there would be no need for the atonement (For all have sinned...Romans 3:23).

SPIRITUAL HOME TRAINING OF THE CHILD

What is child training? Child training has been defined by someone as the means by which we lovingly help the child through self-discovery, guidance, encouragement, and by example develop the potential in his total personality to become a responsible and mature human being for the glory of God. What a task parents have placed before them!

What is the Scriptural basis for child training? Three primary scripture references help summarize the task. In Deuteronomy 6:4-25 we read that parents are to teach their children in every area of family living - when they sit, walk, lie down, and rise up! Parents need to take every opportunity, when they are driving in the car, taking a walk, going to church, to talk about the things of God and to train them. As covered previously, Proverbs 22:6 states that parents are to train children in the way they should go and when the children are older they will not depart from what they have been taught. This does not guarantee, however, that they will become Christians. It does mean that the basic values and beliefs that have been taught early in childhood will remain with them till their dying day.

In Mark 10:13-16 Jesus rebuked the disciples for not taking time with children. He used a child as an example to the disciples that adults must come as little children by faith to inherit the Kingdom of God.

Finally, in Ephesians 6:4 parents are not to provoke their children to anger, but to bring them up in the nurture (love) discipline (instruction) of the Lord. A major problem seen with younger children is that when over-corrected they become discouraged. Discouraged children tend to do poorly in school, and in every other area of life. Children need encouragement, not to be provoked to anger but to be encouraged, nurtured and disciplined or trained in the principles of God and His love.

So why is child training so significant? Why can't children just raise themselves? Children by nature are self-centered. They are absorbed with themselves and their desires.

Children must be taught while they are young, easily moldable and pliable. Furthermore, we must counteract regressive philosophies that are so apparent today, as seen in television, radio, the internet on bill boards, and within the school system.

These philosophies imply that sensuality and materialism are to be sought above all else. Self-control or personal restraint is seen as unnatural and unlikely, so the best we can hope for is to provide "safe" expressions for self-absorbed behavior. How contrary to Jesus' teaching that we are to love God and our neighbor with equal fervor.

We must furthermore provide guidance and direction to children in need. When we have problems with our children (and, by the way, problems are inevitable), it is so vitally important that we give them direction and hope. Children are quite vulnerable, and very resilient. We want to teach them early to have a basic trust in God and a positive hope for their future. They need our blessings.

So when does child training really begin? Child training begins at the moment of birth - from the very first bonding that occurs between the mother, father and child, until they leave the nest, and beyond. We are responsible for the training of our children. The school and the church are merely supplemental trainers. Not only are we to train them, but with God's help we have the ability to train effectively and graciously, according to the Lord's plan.

DEVELOPMENTAL TASKS OF CHILDREN

Children develop at their own pace and time, physically, mentally, emotionally, and spiritually. We have learned from research done by human behavior specialists that children develop within general frameworks or in certain developmental phases. In this section we look at developmental phases and generally recognized normal patterns of behavior. It is important to remember, however, that all children are different and that these developmental tasks will be accomplished within certain time frames, although those time frames are rather fluid, not fixed in concrete.

If one can become reasonably familiar with the needs of a child in each developmental stage and patiently adjust his communication with his/her child accordingly, one should be able to avoid unnecessary aggravation and arrive at a dynamic relationship that is healthy for the child and satisfying for the parent.

One of the primary theorists in the field of psychological development is Eric Erickson. Mr. Erickson defined the basic developmental tasks essential to productive living and assigns their accomplishments to specific age periods. As noted above, however, these periods need to be as one observes and interacts with an individual child. Below are listed the developmental milestones for children. They are reviewed in brief to provide an introduction to this important topic.

As you think of your child, try to imagine the unborn child as a gift of God to remind you of His miracle of life. Remember that the child's physical, mental, emotional and spiritual capacities will be unfolding in a rather predictable pattern over a period of approximately 18 years. Even though we view this 18 year pattern as the completion of the major developmental phases, development continues throughout the entirety of life. In fact, we are now aware that most identity development is finally completed by approximately age 30.

When the infant is born, it is born frightened and needs a significant amount of affection and tender loving care. The child carries an innate fear of the birth experience.

A baby's skin is most sensitive. The baby can sense the muscle tone of the person holding the child. If that individual is tense, the child will relate to the holding with a sense of anxiety. Cuddling while feeding will build emotional health. It is important to understand that a relaxed, caring approach to ones children can facilitate healthy relationships.

Birth to Two Years of Age - During this time the child is attempting to acquire a sense of basic trust while overcoming a sense of mistrust, which develops hope within the child. During this time the child should be seen on a regular basis by a concerned and competent pediatrician. The comfort of the child should be maximized while issues of fear and uncertainty should be minimized. It is important to develop a stable nurturing environment for the child to live in. The child's parent's faith and conviction assures the child's basic trust of the unknown. There is certain evidence of this social trust as seen in the child's ability to feed with a sense of comfort, their depth of sleep, relaxed bowels, and the ability to tolerate limited amounts of mother's absence. These are evidences of the child's positive emotional development and health.

At approximately the age of three, the child begins to develop a sense of autonomy or freedom versus a sense of doubt and shame. The child realizes that he/she has a will of their own. During this time, self care begins to become important to the child. By age three they should be able to feed themselves reasonably well, be able to begin walking and talking, which results in the child's feeling a sense of autonomy from the mother.

Second, toilet training should be accomplished by this time. To do so requires sphincter control, the ability to communicate with speech, and the desire to stop what parents see as the nastiest of habits.

During this time play assumes a most important role in re-establishing the child's balance of power. There is also a new found freedom from the mother often combined with a new brother or sister which produces a necessity for healthy discipline which needs to be fair, firm, and friendly. The family begins to lose a certain amount of control of the child at about age three. The child specifically needs maternal care during the first three years of life.

Beginning at approximately age four or five, the child begins to acquire a need for initiative verses an overwhelming sense of guilt. That is, they begin to realize purpose for their life. During this time the child intrudes into the space of others, which often results in feelings of discomfort and guilt. When a child begins to break away from mom, which is the best time to introduce the concept of God. Jesus as God should be introduced to the child as a friend. God will love you no matter where you live, what your color is, what your background is. God is a friend to children. He loves you just the way you are. This is vitally important for children of this age to hear and understand. The child is asked to assume responsibility for themselves on a limited basis. As needed, physical discipline should begin. Physical discipline is a paralanguage necessity. Limits need to be internalized by the child which will only occur as external limits are provided by parents. His/her conscience becomes increasingly important and will assume the role of the parent when they are away from the parent. At no time is the child ready to learn or to relate cooperatively with others. That will come at a later date.

From ages six through approximately eleven, the acquiring of a sense of industry versus inferiority is most important. Doing helps the child realize a sense of competence. Before the child can become an adult, he must learn to be a worker. As she/he realizes that he is neither capable nor invited to take an equal part in the adult world, the child is pressured to move more and more into their peer world. This has positive and negative ramifications.

Furthermore, the child will work to resolve feelings of inferiority by culturally mandated skills. Successful negotiation of theses skills occur through successfully competing with his peers. Finally, the child begins to compare his parents with other adults.

During these stages, the family remains the most powerful influence in the life of the child. Beginning around age eight to eleven, peers become increasingly important. Jocehbed and Hannah demonstrated how deeply parents can influence the early years of a child's life. The example of Moses and Samuel ought to elevate in a parent's mind the importance of good child/parent relationships during the preschool years.

ENTERING YOUR TEEN'S WORLD

If you make a careful examination of Scripture, you will see that there has always been a certain distance between generations. Because of the explosive scientific and technological advances of our age, the post-war era has been most difficult. This can especially be seen in the lives of teenagers. Parents and their children probably experience an exaggerated pressure upon their relationship, but there is little to indicate that this will be a permanent phenomenon of our culture. Whether or not this gap is closed will depend largely upon the degree to which each set of parents and teens want to bridge it. Remember that bridges are built from both sides. Perhaps bridge building can be encouraged by a clear understanding of what is going on in the young person's life.

With that in mind, let us look at the development of a teenager beginning with the first stage, ages **twelve through fourteen**. During this time the teenager is attempting to acquire a sense of identity while overcoming identity confusion, while realizing a sense of fidelity for his or her life. There are many important physiological changes which occur because of the rapid body growth of an adolescent. This growth threatens the person's previously learned trust in his or her own body. For this reason there is often a preoccupation with the body and physical appearance for the adolescent. There is significant comparison done amongst the peer group to try to fit in to the way others look. Youth is now searching for something to believe in, someone to whom he/she can be true.

From ages **fifteen through eighteen**, there is an attempt to acquire a sense of intimacy and avoid a sense of isolation realizing love. Most teens acquire the capacity for healthy adulthood and must now be demonstrated by the ability to love and work. The chronological criteria for adulthood in this case are very inadequate. Developmental criteria suggests that a person is an adult when they can be responsible, act as an adult, are able to be responsible for themselves, for a mate, for offspring and to his/her community.

During recent times and due to the change in economics, this is not quite as true as before. Nowadays true adulthood has been delayed into the early or even late twenties, whereas one generation ago it was by sixteen that most young men and young women were actively seeking adulthood.

By ages **eighteen through adulthood** there is the acquiring of a sense of creativity while avoiding self-absorption, realizing the care of others. A healthy marriage relationship is a foundation for assuring the care and satisfactory development of the next generation.
The second phase of adulthood involves creativity versus stagnation. This includes a sense of parental responsibility toward community.

DISCOVERY

An expanding social world presents the young person with an increasing number of opportunities for experiences that will test his/her value system. There are two primary fears that characterize this relationship. First of all, the young person fears that the parent won't permit him/her enough liberty or freedom to become an individual in his or her own right. Secondly, the parent fears the young person will become so different from his/her parents with his/her new liberty that they will become strangers. You may have noticed that clothes, language and music fads appear in great measure during this time. It is therefore wise for the parents to strike a balance between supervision and basic trust in their relationship.

With this in mind, it is noted that tension and conflict are a normal part of the parent-teen relationship. The ultimate goal is to successfully launch a new life into the adult community which is usually accompanied by both the young person and his parents experiencing the twin feelings of relief and satisfaction. Where that is not accomplished, we can see one of two things; either the child never fully realizing their ability to leave the home and therefore being inadequately developed as an adult, or where the tensions increase to too great a measure and a child may be sent out of the home before they are actually ready. This sets up a series of failures that will negatively affect the child the rest of his life. It is a very important phase of development for all young people.

The years between **fifteen and twenty-five** form life's decade of decision. During these years young people make the **three most important decisions of their lives.**[11] They make a decision about **their faith**, as noted by studies that indicate that most people choose their values when they are between eighteen and twenty-one years of age. A companion statistic to that is that most conversions occur between sixteen and twenty-one years of age.

Furthermore, they determine their **life's work**. What are they going to do for the next few years of their life; how are they going to perform; in what direction are they going to

---

[11] Assistance for parents, designed to help youth make healthy decisions can be found in Dr. DeKoven's book, *From a Fathers Heart.*

go. This is truly a major decision. And thirdly, and certainly not least, is a decision about **their mate**. The truth is that too many marriages are prematurely precipitated by an over-heated relationship or by an unconscious need to leave the family or to find that one person that is "going to fulfill all of my needs." A person is less apt to be hurt by the mate selection process if he understands the process and if they have developed positive and healthy relationships within the family of origin. The remainder of life may be viewed as living out the consequences of these decisions. This is, in some cases, unfortunate, however it is quite true.

CONCLUSIONS

Launching young people into life involves its anxious moments for everyone. It is important to remember the story of the prodigal son which should help us to avoid unnecessary condemnation of parents or young people when painful detours delay the onset of mature adult living.

It is hoped that understanding more about what goes on between generations will help to alleviate some fears and make this transitional period more fulfilling for both generations.

DISCIPLINE

Discipline is one of the most difficult areas for parents to deal with. In this section we will develop some guidelines for children in regard to discipline. Please understand that this is not the ultimate authority in child discipline, but only guidelines in handling your children.

The purpose of discipline is to establish guidelines of expected behavior and to shape positive or good and behavior and minimize negative or wrong behavior. A parent's goal is to train children in a healthy direction, as stated in Proverbs 22:6.

In Hebrews chapter 12 it states that without discipline we cannot really know the love of God. There are many expectations that we have of children. Some parents expect that children should be seen and not heard, that children are to be protected but not trusted. But children need active, hands on parents. It is important that we discipline our children. Discipline is needed; the how of discipline depends upon the child and the situation where discipline is needed. In either case, parents are called upon to encourage and support their children as they grow through the difficult transitions of life.

Of course, rules for children are needed, with a goal of teaching children to obey God by trying their best in what they do (II Tim. 2:15). Furthermore, children are to obey their parents (Eph. 6:1). Also, it is important to teach children to obey legitimate authorities, such as teachers, Sunday school teachers, pastors, policemen, etc. We are not talking about blind obedience, but we do need to teach them the difference between right and wrong, between good and bad. Nonetheless, we need to teach them healthy respect, which is done through discipline when they are disrespectful. Children need to be taught to take care of other people's property and respect boundaries. This is accomplished through children demonstrating respect for property within homes, for property within the church, and by not allowing the children to run wild in supermarkets, in church, at home, etc. (I John 4:7-8).

Furthermore, children are to be taught to help one another. Selfishness is one of the biggest problems in children. The inability to share, issues of jealously and discipline will help to remove the childish characteristics of jealousy and the inability to share to a great extent (Eph. 4:32, I Cor. 6:1-11). As a child grows, it is important to recognize that their needs and the style of discipline necessary for them changes. In general, children need to learn that there are natural and logical consequences for their behaviors. Should a rule be broken by a child, whoever is the closest parent should be the one to make the correction. When a child caught doing something wrong, parents must lovingly, but firmly reprimand them. If necessary, especially if they are under age 7-8, a spanking can be the most appropriate way to impact the negative/defiant behavior. Spanking was designed for the rear end and no other place.

If misbehavior continues, or defiant behavior occurs, spanking is more appropriate than at any other time. Up to the place of defiance, talking to the child (not lecturing, but talking to them), using "time out" (1 minute for each year of age up to age 8) or removing a privilege is often most appropriate.

After age 7-8 and beyond, natural and logical consequences seem to work best. An example of that would be if your child is unable to clean their room, rather than a spanking they need to learn to clean more effectively. Not only would they have to clean their room, they would have to clean other things to remind them of their need to be responsible. Another example would be if they break something, not only do they have to clean up the mess, but they have to replace it as well. That is, making restitution. If they cannot afford to replace it, they may have an assigned job as a way of restitution for what has been broken.

In summary, here are some guidelines for discipline. From ages 0-2, immediate physical discipline, as in a slap on the hand or the rear end, with a firm "no, no", should be sufficient. From ages 2-7 or 8, spanking is permitted, but not mandatory, followed by the reason for the discipline and prayer for forgiveness. It is important that parents model God's grace as well as His judgment. By ages 8-18, discipline to fit the crime such as work jobs, writing sentences, restrictions, Bible lessons in the area of the problem, essays....the list is only limited by a parent's creativity.

CORPORAL PUNISHMENT CONTINUED

There are many ways to discipline. Proverbs 17:10 says that "a rebuke goes deeper into one who has understanding than a hundred blows into a fool." A child who has understanding can be dealt with and trained. Proverbs 19:25 says, "strike a scoffer and the naive may become shrewd, but reprove one who has understanding and he will gain knowledge." When a child has done something wrong, we can also train them from the Word of God. Proverbs 14:2 tells us that "he who walks in uprightness fears the Lord, but he who is crooked in his way despises the Lord."

Corporal punishment should be used as a last resort. Proverbs 15:10 says that "stern discipline is for him who forsakes the way, for he who hates reproof will die." Corporal punishment is for the fool. Proverbs 26:3 says, "a whip is for the horse, a bridle for the donkey, and a rod for the back of fools." The Bible clearly says that to spare the rod will spoil the child. The original Hebrew word for "rod" means discipline. Spare discipline and you will clearly spoil your child. The form of discipline is not nearly as important as discipline itself.

In regards to corporal punishment, make a distinction between discipline and corporal punishment. Too many parents spank on impulse. They react to a child's behavior, rather than responding reasonably. Doing this is like cutting down a tree without digging out the roots. The tree behavior will only grow back again.

Remember, a child has a built in need for love, attention and approval. The main attention many children receive comes when they are receiving corporal punishment. This will reinforce negative or undesirable behavior. A child may reason that negative attention is better than no attention at all. Another way to deal with negative behavior is to selectively ignore it and only give positive attention, where possible, when the child is doing something desirable, such as sitting quietly, reading a book, being polite, etc. We have to learn to catch our children doing things well, and encourage them.

Instead of using corporal punishment, we ought to first use discipline. Proverbs 13:14 says, "The teaching of the wise is a fountain of life to turn aside from the snares of death." We ought to spend time with our children to teach them principles for behavior, not just rules. We should teach them righteousness for Proverbs says that "He who is steadfast in righteousness will attain to life, and he who pursues evil will bring about his own death." We also need to teach them the fear of the Lord for Proverbs 16:6 says,

"By the fear of the Lord, men depart from evil." We all need to learn that you reap what you sow. Some day take them to skid row and show them the "glamour" of drinking, drug, etc. It will have a much more profound effect on them than a lecture. Study the Word with them. Let them see the desirability of righteousness and the wisdom of living godly lives. **Begin to teach them wisdom and understanding with the Holy Spirit's help.**

It would be unrealistic to say that even though we teach our children the fear of the Lord, they will never need correction or discipline. Yet, if parents have instilled the fear of the Lord in children, teaching them wisdom and understanding, discipline will become easier and more effective. Proverbs 15:32-33 says that "he who neglects discipline despises himself, but he who listens to reproof acquires understanding." The time we spend disciplining our children should be a time of instruction.

ADOLESCENCE AND FAMMILY LIFE

Mark Twain wrote a story that is quoted something like this, "When a child reaches age 13, that is, when they become an adolescent, the best thing that a parent can do is to put the child into an apple barrel, put the lid on tightly, and feed the child through the hole in the barrel. Then, when the child reaches 16, plug up the hole!" It is unlikely that Twain was serious in his intent, yet how many parents have felt the same type of frustration or sense of hopelessness in dealing with teenagers.

In counseling troubled teens over many years I have found them to be most fascinating characters. Teens are really caught between transitioning worlds. Their world vacillates between one of a child, dependent upon parents, and of young adults, wishing for independence and freedom from their family of origin. This normal struggle is common to all teens to one degree of another. What most parents need is to gain practical insights and basic principles of helping teens in transition, while remaining sane in the family. Teens can be most difficult to work with, but also a tremendous joy.

First and foremost, it is essential that parents lay the foundation of discipline or self-control (child training and spiritual training) early in the child's life. This must be built with loving sensitivity. Since teenagers are no longer little children, but are growing to maturity, a parent's tactics or care towards them must be modified. Adolescents require a certain amount of independence, freedom, and an increase in the level of responsibility for their actions. Telling a teen "no" and 'because I said so" is no longer an effective deterrent to them. Parents must lean to modify previous authoritarian patterns (if previously used) and become a coach or mentor to remain effective.

It is such a difficult balancing act for most parents to determine how much freedom and how much responsibility is necessary for their teen. The only reasonable guideline is that every teenager is a bit different. Thus, parent's need the sensitivity of the Holy Spirit and reasoned common sense.

Teenagers need, and deserve their right to privacy so they can be alone if necessary or desirable. At the same time, if a teenager withdraws from family life, as well as from friends, concerned caution is warranted. Having special family times will provided needed accountability; at the same time recognize that teenagers need time for themselves. The more responsibility you give in areas of family life and for decisions about their future life, the better. They need guidance in all areas, but can also benefit by being allowed to make decisions, even in making mistakes.

Adolescents still require reasonable, negotiated boundaries that they must adhere to. They require a minimum of rules and regulations to follow. Along with basic rules, they need specific responsibilities assigned to them within the household that are appropriate for their age, time, etc.

The building of a positive self-image for teens is essential. During adolescence teenagers are trying to find themselves. They are asking the difficult questions of "Who am I," "Where do I fit into the world," and "What am I going to do with my life?" A positive self-image and sense of personal worth, along with an acknowledgement of their importance or significance in the world helps greatly. A healthy self-image can be developed through various means, such as specific accomplishments and successes, but ultimately is to be rooted in relationship with Christ and significant others, including parents.

Adolescents are to attend school and church functions, which are primarily oriented towards their peer group. It is important that parents take an interest in what they are doing in school in a positive way. Furthermore, parents are wise to get to know their teen's friends, because peers tend to influence teenagers more than parents do. Remember, when teenagers become older they will not depart from what they have learned if we have laid a good foundation based upon God's Word. However, great patience and much prayer can help us during a potentially rocky transition.

In talking to teens, and especially when disciplining them, integrating principles and commands from God's Word in informal conversations can make impact. Adults often fear relating to teenagers, and yet the language difficulties are not that hard to break through. Do not preach at your emerging adults, but instead listen to them actively. Try to understand their perceptions and needs. It is worth every effort to converse with teens. Eventually, adulthood will come and having had open communication during the teen years lead to a more satisfying adult relationship.

CHURCH AND FAMILY

All adult leaders must practice what we preach and teach to our children. Teen-agers are excellent schoolyard lawyers. They see every discrepancy and they are going to point it out to us. Their ability to see adult "hypocrisy" has been used to avoid church life for many.

Families should attend church together as a positive, planned activity. Parents must resist the tendency to give children an option, as long as they live in the home, as to whether they participate in church or not. Parents that have given their teenagers that option have later regretted it, as the children become more rebellious towards parents and parental authority.

Having an open home for your teenagers and for their friends is a key to continued communication. Many parents have said, "I don't want my kid's friends over here. They're dirty, they're too loud." Yet, the easiest way to keep an eye on your teens is to have them near with their friends. As you learn about their friends and treat them with respect, your children's friends can become your allies as well. However, do not be one of the gang to your children. Many adults will try to become like their teenagers. This mistake will no doubt backfire. Be a parent to your teenager, which they need and will respect.

Furthermore, parents need to be a source of encouragement to adolescents. Assure them that they are loved and accepted, and make the most of the time that you have with them.

VOCATIONAL GUIDANCE

A special concern in teen development is the choosing of a meaningful vocation. It is inherent upon the parent to be actively involved in vocational guidance. Teens still desire to please their parents. Thus, parents must set the tone in the family for work being positive, not something to be avoided. The work habits that are demonstrated to children, in the home as well as outside, will determine how they to respond to work situations later in life. Good work habits and skills will sustain them over a life time.

Specifically, what can parents do to guide their children vocationally? First and foremost it is important to introduce the child to Christ early in life, for a life of Christian service. Historically, Christian service has meant assuming the ole of a pastor, Christian education director, or an evangelist. Truly full time Christian service means devoting our life to Christ in whatever we do. The world needs fully committed, Christian workers in all vocational areas. Service through work is service to Christ, as we yield our lives to Him in a vocational choice.

Furthermore, we should stress the need to find the will of God for each individual. That happens as we teach and train children. Acquainting children with the wide variety of opportunities in Christian service can be very helpful. It is also wise to evaluate objectively and realistically a child's abilities and interests. This can be done within the school setting through psychological testing or through vocational interest inventories, but often comes via observation and common sense. By listening and talking to children one can determine areas of interest and provide appropriate guidance for them. It is important to help a child realistically ascertain their vocational goals and objectives.

Parents can also provide good literature on different vocational interests. Discussing areas of obvious interest and gifting should then follow. Of course, parents should pray for the Lord to lead in the lives of their children and pray with them as well. There is nothing more frightening to a young man or a woman than to be turning 18 without a goal for the future. It is a time that they specifically need parental support.

Parents can help their teens get acquainted with the different schools available for their children. Bible Institutes and Colleges, Christian Liberal Arts Colleges, vocational schools, etc. are all possible options for vocational preparation. Emphasize that "being" is far more important that "doing." What you are as a human being is much more important than where you go and what you do. As your adolescent begins to work at different schools or jobs, help them to fully evaluate the merits of the job or school in light of their future. Keeping the lines of communication open so that guidance is a natural part of life is very helpful. Furthermore, expressing your opinions about vocations without forcing children to think your way is a very positive move on a parent's part. Children may rebel. Not because of certain preferences that we have, but because they feel forced or pushed into certain vocational areas. Adolescents are becoming young adults and will have to make the choice for their vocational life. A parent's role is to coach, support and guide. Remember, what may be current today may be obsolete tomorrow. Do research as a parent in different vocations and share your findings about them, or at least encourage your teenager to do the same. Show a clear interest in what they want, and be willing to honestly and frankly answer questions pose. It is helpful to provide a personal testimony to your children about how God has led you in your life. Both the highs and the lows, the good and the bad, need to be shared so that our children can learn from our experiences.

WINDS OF CHANGE

Around the time your adolescent reaches 16, most parents begin a time of change some what proportional to the teens change. Some have coined this time of transition a mid life crisis. I prefer the concept of a mid marriage condition. This is necessary due to the following family situations.

First, as parents and children settle into the family routine, the normal (not necessarily healthy or best, just that which most do), focuses of life becomes somewhat fixed. Dad's primary focus and priority is success in business or career. Mom's that of home and hearth.[12]

---

[12] At least stereotypically.

Often, parents will develop a primary bond with one child and the other, a dynamic which will be explored in detail in the counseling section of this book. Suffice it to say that the intimacy once enjoyed by the couple before children is generally long since past. There may or may not be conflict, since the emotional needs of each spouse is being met through their new focus, the child. This may last several years, where the distance (some what unconscious or at least under attended to) develops between the husband and wife increases, until the youngest child reaches the middle teens. This progression of time sets the stage for a major transition, which could be a crisis or an opportunity for significant and satisfying growth.

Briefly, as a couple becomes increasingly aware of their youngest child's independence from mom and dad, a forced encounter occurs between them. Depending on several factors (the fundamental strength of the marital covenant, the strength of attachment to the children, the amount of hurt built up between the couple, the perceived success or failure of the husband) in combination, the couple will move closer or become more distant, grow in deeper love and friendship (often with renewed zest in their romantic life) or slide towards emotional or even physical divorce.

IT AIN'T ALL BAD

In fact, if faced with open hearts and active communication, most parents make this transition with grace. My wife and I began planning for our emancipation when we were first parents. We had two wonderful daughters, and though we could look back and see mistakes made, we reconciled to the fact that we had done our best. Where we failed, we sought reconciliation. We actually looked forward (prayerfully) to their college years, marriage and grand parenting (our ultimate revenge, though we were in no hurry!)

It is most important for the church and specifically leaders to be aware of this very difficult transition, and be prepared to assist in the process. Many sad and painful decisions can be avoided with proper education and guidance.

OLDER AND BETTER

Western society is painfully and obviously youth oriented, to the detriment of the elderly. The pursuit of personal comfort and materialism has had devastating consequences for our elderly. Rather than being honored and revered, they are frequently marginalized, dishonored and abandoned. This truly is a uniquely Western phenomena, since most Eastern and Two-third world cultures have great respect for the elderly.

There are many challenges and difficult decisions that may need to be made as parents grow into their twilight years. Listed here are some of the many concerns/considerations with brief though totally biased commentary.

THE GOOD

Having been loosed from the confines of parenting, (except to spoil the grandkids and send them home) and, if they have been fiscally wise, and in reasonable health, parents reaching their mid 50's and beyond can and should enjoy the fruit of their labor. Generally, the major struggles to provide house and home are over, and there is a wonderful freedom to be and do, for self and the Kingdom. One of our greatest material resources is the wisdom, assistance and wealth of the 55+.

Conversely, if the parents have been less successful (or unsuccessful), this can lead to other decisions regarding the care of parents, possible supplementation to income, or even nursing care. That is why I use and strongly recommend a Christian, well trained financial planner to assist in contingency planning.

During this later phase of life, the main preoccupation for adults is the preservation of the family, the finalization or summing up of one's life. Open discussion regarding finances, death, should be encouraged, rejoiced in and planned for, as a natural extension of life.

The writer of Ecclesiastes states that there is a time and season for everything. (Eccl. 3:1) As we recognize God's hand in each season, and work to cooperate with Him and each other in growth, we are able to fulfill God's plan. Perhaps this is the reason Jesus emphasized the Kingdom of God and His righteousness, and that all things needed, regardless of our age in years, will be added to us.

THE FAMILY AND REST

When I was first introduced into Youth for Christ/Campus Life, I was already a committed Christian. As a "holiness" oriented believer I had been fully indoctrinated in the Protestant work ethic, in striving for perfection, and in obsessive-compulsive activity which was supposed to lead to growth in the Lord. My assumption from church training (much of which was quite good, especially regarding discipline, consistency, persistence, etc.) was that to be successful as a Christian meant all work and no play. As with large segments of Christians, my worth was directly related to my performance, both in terms of my relationship with my fellow man and God. The performance treadmill adversely affects our ability to "be" and "know" God or others. Beginning with Youth for Christ (though by "no" means instantaneous) a paradigm shift began which has been a positive influence and growing revelation.

THE BALANCE OF LIFE

Since God has made us whole people (spirit, soul and body) and all three are needed for life here on earth, living life in harmony with God, self, others and the world is essential for happiness. Campus life put this into a simplified formula. Our tripartite being must function in harmony in four primary areas, physical (individual health habits, physical exercise, sleep, nutrition); mental (individual education, preparation for vocation); social (which encompasses recreation, relationships) and spiritual (spiritual discipline such as church, prayer, Bible study, intercession, etc.). Although it is acknowledged that all four arenas develop at different rates, and at different times one may have greater emphasis than another, our lives must strike a balance of sorts in each of these areas for health and happiness. Even Jesus developed in similar fashion. (Luke 2:52). If it was good enough for Christ, it must be for us! As a counselor, it is fairly easy to diagnosis a problem when one is out of balance in one or more of these areas. The tragedy often seen in Christendom is the over or under emphasis on any of these areas. Let me explain further.

LET GEORGE DO IT

In church growth circles the 80/20 rule is often discussed. That is, 20% of the people in a local assembly will do 80% of the work, 80% will do 20%. This is paralleled in giving, devotional life, etc...

The solution to the "Let George" or someone else do it crowd, is not to whip the people into a frenzy of guilt. However, balance must be sought (no easy task, if I had the secret formula, I'd be world famous!) between the doers and observers, the workers and the want-to-bees. The goal is to live to the best of our ability in balance within the described arenas, for being out of balance (all things in moderation, Phil. 4:5) cause our primary dysfunctions. If someone has total devotion to their physical life, the spiritual, social and mental can be neglected, if spiritual life is the one and only life, they can become so spiritually minded they will become no earthly good. However, the lack of balance in the life of Christian people manifested most when it comes to rest and recreation.

REST - GOD'S IDEA

In God's word we read that we are to labor 6 days, with the 7th being a day of rest (Ex. 20:8-11). We can hardly call Sunday a day of rest, and thus, for many of us, we rarely take the time for necessary inactivity or rest from all laborers (including our Saturday football, basketball, baseball, reclamation of our youth).

Even Christ had to rest, and instructed His disciples to do the same, inspite of the needs of humanity (Mark 6:30). God created us with a need for recuperative rest, which can be done in a number of ways, unique to the individual and family. For some, a good book and soft music is ideal, for others, a hard game of racquetball or work out at the gym. Most likely, especially in light of family life, recreation that satisfies individual and group is as difficult to find as personal balance, but is no less important.

IT'S THE CHANGE THAT MATTERS

Most of our lives are intently routine; washing, school, homework, some social time, church, chores, all within the confines of a standard week. Taking a break from the routine of life could include:

Physical activity; such as a family walk, bike ride, bowling, or other group activity that is good for the body and soul. Our body is the temple of the Holy Spirit and deserves care (I Cor. 3:16,17) and exercise does profit a little (I Tim. 4:8). Second only to a family meal and church attendance (if non-segregated), physical activity for exercise and fun is a true family builder. Leisure requires a change in activity. Thus, camping (as a family), fishing, etc..., can be great diversions which will provide necessary refreshing.

Also, Social times are essential. In Old Testament times, and even in Jesus' day, feasts and festivals were of great importance. Each were times of remembrance of past victories, and of gratitude for God's blessings. Similar to that would be our modern day celebrations of birthdays, anniversaries, national holidays, weddings, etc. As families, these should also be times of refreshing, fun, sharing, and remembering of God's goodness, grace and mercy. Thus where possible, these can also include the fellowship of believers.

Parenting, from birth to grand children provide opportunity for some of the greatest joy in life. Preparing for this most important role in life needs to be emphasized early and throughout the various stages of the cycle of life.

"The Lord certainly knew what he was doing when He gave small children to young couples."
Author Unknown

MEDIA AND THE FAMILY

Unfortunately, for most western families the primary point of togetherness is found around the television.

Television, internet, ipods, etc., can be tools for fun and entertainment, or used to avoid and undermine family life. It is incumbent upon parents to be responsible for what their children and/or adolescents ingest through various media. There are advantages, limitations, and questions that should be asked self in regards to media consumption.

First, there are certain advantages. Media can be a way to broaden our world and encourage intellectual development. Furthermore, it can build vocabulary and enrich us in terms of greater awareness of the world in which we live. For many it can lay a basic foundation for education, to include advance learning for younger children. It helps us to be current, especially if we watch the news. It gives us a view of other cultures and ways of life and can provide entertainment and recreation. Television especially can be a means for reaching the masses and can give us historical information - makes the past live and preserves our many traditions. Sometimes these tools can save us time in travel and money. It provides us first viewing of special events that we might not otherwise be able to see.

As with the advantages, of course, there are many limitations or disadvantages that may be found in existing media. First, an over usage of media may lessen the spiritual atmosphere in the home. Media is definitely a secular influence for the most part. I wish we could say that on Christian stations it is always positive, beneficial, and spiritual, but that is not always the case. Television, internet and music can affect study habits and negatively impact reading skills in children. Furthermore, it can be a source of irritation and disagreement in families. It often hinders communication, family interaction and unity because it makes passive listeners and thinkers of the whole family. It can affect our total living pattern; it interrupts and distracts. It influences our morals, even affects our attitudes and reactions toward sin, crime, and violence as it desensitizes us to the reality of the moral climate. Children often watch a character murdered on television or in a video, only to see them back on television the next week in a different soap opera or television program. This can certainly distort the reality of life.

Media can waste precious time, which could be used for more constructive things as a family. It is a soft medium designed to encourage consumerism and materialism, which has become the god of West. Furthermore, video games and Television can teach and/or reinforce aggressive behavior in certain children, making it more difficult and challenging to create interest in learning.

WHAT IS A PARENT TO DO?

If you have television/internet, etc. in your home, you may want to answer some of the following questions. It may help you determine whether or not media used in your home is a problem.

First, does your T.V./video games/ipods, etc., disrupt your meals? Does the dialogue learned there intrude on live conversations? Do you arrange your household chores around television viewing? Has the internet crowded out a hobby, family devotions, or do it yourself projects around your home? Has it interrupted a visit with friends or neighbors? Do video games cause you to be late for a meeting, or just stay home? Does your family have to compete for attention? Does it keep you from getting the sleep that you need? Furthermore, does it desensitize your actions towards violence or other forms of immorality?

If any of these statements are true of your home, you may want to reevaluate the amount and quality of media usage you do and the priority it has in your life. There are certain principles to observe in watching television. They include:

- Choose television programs carefully. Screen what is to be or not to be watched. Use filters for the internet to insure that inappropriate material is not available for the family, especially children.
- Require priorities to be cared for first; such things as studies for school, responsibilities around the home and toward one another, personal needs certainly should be more important than personal entertainment.
- Turn off the T.V. when company is coming or when you want to concentrate on important things as a family.
- Allow only a certain number of programs and limit internet and video time, if allowed, to be seen in any given day and require that your children earn to make choices about what they are going to view. That will make them discriminative media consumers in the future.

- Do not hesitate to eliminate a form of media that is morally offensive. Be aware of your morally sensitive areas, and those of your children. Remember your children need to be protected from the polluting influence of the outside world.
- Watch programs with your children and discuss what you see - use them as an opportunity for constructive dialog.
- Write to stations or sponsors if you are dissatisfied with what you have seen. Believe it or not, public outcries against certain types of programming can make a difference.

CONCLUSION

Every facet of our life together as a family unit is important and deserves attention. Seek for balance since there are few if any hard and fast rules of engagement. Let love and God's word be your primary guides.

KEEPING THE FAMILY TOGETHER

Happy and healthy families are not perfect homes. In reality, conflict in relationships is inevitable. However, there are some characteristics of families, which describe themselves as successful which bear repeating and commentary. Before looking at these in same detail, it is important to acknowledge God's plan for building a house. Two primary scriptures apply, Ps. 127:1 and Prov. 24:3-4.

THE LORD MUST BUILD THE HOUSE

Ps. 127:1 states "unless the Lord builds the house, they labor in vain who build it, unless the Lord guards the city, the watchman keeps awake in vain."

From conception to emancipation, from dependence to independence (the normal process) it takes the help of the Lord to build a family. In past times, where roles were clear and explicit, family life was relatively simple. In our highly diverse and technological society, family life is intensely complex. Though complex the basic need for love and security for each family member remains constant. We must have the Lord as our family leader and His divine protection, lest we build a family in our image devoid of His blessing and purpose. We must build the house using three primary components found in God's word, wisdom, understanding, and knowledge.

Proverbs 24:3,4, *"By wisdom a house is built, and by understanding it is established; and by knowledge the rooms are filled with all precious and pleasant riches."* These are all cognitive functions requiring thinking. Each area is worth serious consideration.

KNOWLEDGE

Knowledge includes information gleaned through study and experience. This includes study of God's word and solid Christian and/or secular literature. Experience is not always the best teacher. We can learn much from others experience and avoid needless errors in judgment or conduct. However, merely reading and gaining knowledge alone will not guarantee success in family life.

UNDERSTANDING

It is necessary to synthesize what we have learned to be able to make application to daily experience. One can know conceptually about the need for good communication (as will be explored in depth in the next section), but we must understand how to communicate in order to ensure relationship building. Understanding how families work, what the needs of children are, when developmental change can be expected is an essential step towards effective family life. Yet, even if we have knowledge and understanding, we still are ill equipped for family life if we do not apply wisdom.

WISDOM

Wisdom represents the ability to profit from life's experience and to use knowledge and understanding to meet the familiar problems and new situations that impact family relationships. Wisdom, given to us by the Holy Spirit to those who ask, will show us when to apply certain knowledge and understanding to the variety of situations we will likely face in our daily interactions.

Along with these characteristics, we must remember the reality of God's plan for family life. That is, from birth until emancipation (leave and cleave, Gen. 2:24), our children are to grow from total dependence to interdependence or adulthood, where a child becomes a fully functional adult, responsible for their own affairs. As such, the relationship between mom and dad and children must ebb and flow between permission and permissiveness, between active and passive, between control and liberty. That is why parenting is both science and art. We must have God's wisdom to be successful!

THE HEALTHY HOME

In a study conducted by the University of Nebraska several

positive characteristics were found in self reported happy and healthy homes. These characteristics are maintainable in a Christian home, and include:

Unconditional Love, or a sense that no matter what, our love for one another has no limit. In fact, it is precisely because of our love that we feed, clothe, wash, teach, discipline, etc., for the good of others. Also, a healthy home is one which was described as having...

Habitability and Predictability, or an environment that provided a trustworthy and safe environment. Children need to be able to trust before risking in other life tasks.

Thirdly, the healthy family had a good balance between **Freedom and Control**, which was age appropriate. Giving the keys of the car to an eight year old would be to grant freedom for certain, but freedom which would no doubt lead to tragedy (and be simply stupid). However, never allowing your teenager to have friends outside of the home would be too limiting (and equally as fruitless).

Along with age appropriate freedom was added **Age Appropriate Discipline**, which had the focus of teaching rather than punishment. The goal of discipline in healthy families was lesson learning and the teaching of positive family values or of self-discipline and positive self-esteem and conscience building. This was done through consistent rules and their application, as well as positive modeling for children.

The final two areas are linked. They are the ability to **Share Common Goals** and the willingness to Subordinate Personal Goals for the needs of the family (on an equal basis). Healthy families have goals for themselves which are clearly understood by all the members of the Home. These goals are both short term (such as for family vacation, all helping clean the house before leaving on activity), and long term goals like college education for all children, etc. However, when individual goals were in conflict with family goals, there is a willingness to subordinate individual goals for the greater good. Of course, this is not done by only one (as a mom who always sacrifices for others) but by all who are aware of those greater needs. Healthy families were centered on their family life, with a healthy sense of "we" as family and with a knowledge of responsibility to one another.

ENEMIES OF THE FAMILY

The enemies of God are the enemies of the family. Satan has desires to attack and destroy our families, and usually tries to infiltrate from without to destroy from within. Thus, we must be aware of the areas of vulnerability that our families are subject to, and with God's help close these areas of vulnerability to attack and sabotage. The enemies include:

- False teachers and false philosophies espoused by our society at large. We cannot keep our children from humanistic philosophy, but we can counteract it through teaching the truth from God's word. We can not assume that our children are thoroughly indoctrinated if they are in church, Sunday school or Christian Day Schools. They need the Godly influence of parents who "trust in the Lord..." Prov. 3:5-6.

- We must also teach our children to reject sin (and learn to discern what sin is). We must teach our children what to do and what not to do. Flee youthful lust and submit oneself to God, love, forgive and make amends when hurting someone, as well as avoiding the lust of the flesh, eyes, and the pride of life.
- In all things, we are to follow Christ. A good question to ask ourselves (regardless of age or reason of life) is what would Jesus do? We are to pursue God with all our being, and draw to each other as members of His family.

"The fear and the Lord is the beginning of wisdom."
Prov 9:10

COMMUNICATION IN THE FAMILY

There are several functions to appropriate communication within the family. Below is outlined the simple model of communication, which may help you understand why communication problems occur within a family, and what can be done to change them.

One of the major functions of communication is to give a sense of meaning to life. If we do not understand what is being communicated we cannot develop a meaningful relationship. For example, if something is said with context, and responded to in kind, neither party will understand. Even if what is being spoken makes perfect sense to the one doing the speaking, unless the listener understands clearly, communication does not ensue.

To enable us to establish relationships with others is a

primary function of communication. All about us are people we work with, play with, and love. Who are they? How do they think and feel? Will I be able to get along with them? How do I go about it? Communication helps us to answer these meaning filled concerns. There are three simple components to communication. They are Attention, Responding, and Sharing.

ATTENTION

To give or receive a message one must first get someone's attention. It is necessary to give attention to the verbal and non-verbal message. Generally, attention is best gained by simply asking for it, or by calling someone's name and ensuring that you have eye contact has been established or other assurance that attention has been gained. Nothing is more frustrating then to be talking away at your husband or wife, only to hear a "huh, you talkin' to me?" or "Sure honey, whatever" after asking if $100,000.00 is too much to spend on your spring wardrobe!

RESPONDING

Responding to a message requires that it be listened to and understood. Much misunderstanding and conflict occurs as a result of responding to what one "thought" they heard, only to learn that they were responding to the wrong message.

SHARING

Sharing goes beyond daily platitudes or the updating of daily events. Sharing includes the deeper revelations of the heart which provides the atmosphere for intimacy and communication. The process and problems of communication can be seen whenever any of these three areas are not cared for in relationship.

THE PROCESS AND THE PROBLEM

The process usually starts out slowly: "What's your name?": "Where are you from?" "What do you do?" We don't come right out and say, "I'm trying to establish a relationship with you," but that's exactly what we are saying. Communication is the tool which enables us to build relationships. Without it, no relationship is possible. Communication is a vital skill for us to learn and use, but it is often difficult for people to communicate effectively.

One of the major functions of communication is to enable others to establish relationships with us. This is the reverse of the point just made. The responsibility is on us as others try to establish a relationship with us. If we are unwilling to share something of ourselves with others, if we refuse to communicate, we remain strangers.

Sometimes we can make communication difficult for others deliberately; maybe it is a person we do not want to relate to. Maybe we do not like their looks or style, or for some reason we do not trust them. So we "clam up" and turn down the temperature - he/she gets the "cold shoulder." Or maybe we don't really know how to communicate at all. We have never been able to go deeper than the intellectual or superficial level of conversation with another person, to share not only thoughts, but feelings, fears, failures, hopes and dreams, too.

Or perhaps you only communicate to a certain point. Maybe there are some areas of yourself you don't want the other person to know about, so you are always careful to put your best foot forward to try to make a good impression.

In all these ways we make it difficult for others to establish a relationship with us, by blocking communication.

Another major function of communication is to help us to solve problems. Every human being has problems that we have difficulty solving alone. "Two heads are better than one" - unless both of them are blockheads; and "a problem shared is a problem halved."

Communication helps people with problems benefit from the experience of others who have had similar problems, and have solved them.

TYPES OF COMMUNICATION

There are different types of communication, each with its inherent challenges.

The first and the most readily used form of communication is verbal. Talking to one another, and hopefully listening. A second form is non-verbal, which can include body language, things that we read, things we hear or perhaps, think we hear. An example of non-verbal communication would be the person who is sitting in the pew with his eyes closed and his head bouncing up and down, when later asked how he felt about the sermon says, "Oh, it was wonderful Pastor" when all along you could see that he was somewhere else during the sermon time.

Another form of communication is symbolic, which may include signs, marks, symbols, etc. They can include verbal, such as "Hey" which has many meanings. They can include non-verbal, such as an "O.K." sign. Or, they can be just purely symbolic...something that reminds us of things formerly shared. Another form of communication is empathic listening, or empathic communication. This form of communication is a sharing of thoughts and ideas with a "feeling tone" or on a "feeling level." This form of communication is concerned with the feelings behind the words or the symbols. An example would be that, a shrug of the shoulder, which could mean "I don't know," or "I don't care." We never know until we ask.

It is definitely true that "it's not what you say but how you say it that counts" in communication. Real communication does not take place when it is pure intellectualizing - the basic question remains, "How is he really feeling, behind the words he is using to express it?" This is one of the major problems with communication in families and marriages - when there seems to be two conflicting messages being spoken at the same time. Invariably we call that a double bind message - where there seems to be two statements with one saying, "I care," and the other "I'm angry." The verbal "I care" message could be "I really care about you", while the non verbal statement of "I am angry" is expressed in the shaking their fist. That is a confusing message, and the receiver of the message does not know clearly which one the person means. This happens in families all the time. We will discuss this more under Barriers to Communication.

How the person feels helps us not only to understand what he is saying but what kind of person he is. So, when we listen to the feeling tone, we are able to get closer to the person. Empathic communication produces a warm and open flow between people. The participants have the feeling that they are not being understood, respected, and appreciated. Empathic listening is what we need more of within families and the church.

BARRIERS TO COMMUNICATION

There are many potential barriers to communication. Here are several which will hopefully teach you some ways to improve your communication in marriage and the family.

One of the first barriers in communication is simply **language**. There is always the semantics problem - words meaning different things to different people. A prime example is the over used word "love", which means only sex to the disciples of the Playboy philosophy, but to Christians it means a world of other things: affection, consideration, tenderness, concern, unselfishness, sharing, openness, trust, and faithfulness. "Love" can have very different meanings: "I love you, now come to bed with me," or "I love you, and what can I do for you?" There is also, of course, the obvious problem of different tongues or languages, potentially problematic in interracial or international marriages. It is certainly a problem that can be overcome if people are willing to work at it.

Another barrier to communication is **images**. Words create images which convey certain emotion-charged meanings. For example, one young lady, all mixed up about God, became enraged when told by her counselor to think of Him as a father - because her own father was a drunken abuser of both her and her mother. Therefore, we must be careful in the usage of word, and must insure that both parties area in agreement with the a specific words image.

Defense mechanisms can be another barrier to clear communication. We all have, and must have, defense mechanisms to preserve our integrity and sense of worth. These mechanisms can also block good communication. We employ a wide range of them. Sleeping, doodling, whittling are also forms of defense mechanisms we employ when we do not wish to communicate with another person.

Further, a major barrier to communication is **anxiety** about life and ourselves. It has been said that we live in the age of anxiety. Anxiety, another word for fear, can shut out the other person. When we are afraid, depressed, or confused, we may talk but we will not be able to communicate. We have other needs, more pressing at the moment, and communication is not something we are particularly interested in. In the simple model of effective communication discussed later, we call this a distortion caused by anxiety "noise."

Often people can be at **cross purposes** in their communication. An example of this is the minister who is so dedicated to his work that his wife and family are neglected. His wife may become resentful, hostile, and dissatisfied. He communicates his devotion to family, but by actions communicates something entirely different.

Or perhaps the problem is **ego**; one or both partners may have such a monumental ego that they cannot achieve truly mutual goals. They find themselves at odds about everything, because one or both insist on being right about everything.

Other assorted, not as important but still barriers to communication include:

- Mechanical (noisy environment, need of a hearing aid, etc.)
- Physical condition of the communicators can make a difference. Physical illness may hinder good communication.
- Timing - we must learn to know when and when not to broach a subject. It is not productive to attempt a serious conversation when the other person's not feeling well, when the kids are underfoot, or the husband is just getting ready to leave for work in the morning.
- Pain (both physical and emotional) - when a person's feelings are overwhelmed, positive communication becomes difficult.
- Lack of desire to communicate can be major barrier, especially in marriage. That is, when a person feels no need to change and is perfectly content with him/herself and with the situation just as it is. They will not make an effort to communicate.

DISTORTIONS IN COMMUNICATION

Not only are there barriers to communication, but there are many distortions that may occur. Some of these distortions include using the wrong label. The wife may disagree with me, and I may be tempted to call her "stupid," but really, she's not stupid, she's just "stubborn" and/or "opinionated" (or perhaps right!).

Other labels people use may include such disrespectful labels as "the N word," "red-neck," "wop," "spic," "kike," and "honky." Labels such are deadly to communication because they illicit angry and defensive emotional reactions.

Another distortion in communication is exaggerating the difference between things. This is making mountains out of molehills, like: "She squeezes the toothpaste in the middle! I want a divorce." Or, "He leaves lights on all over the house! I can't live with him any more!"

Often distortion in communication occurs when differing interpretations in taste, dress, interests, habits, etc., are interpreted as indications of a lack of love, making a federal case out of them.

Another distortion is mistaking similarities. Some typical examples of this may include "You're just like your old lady," or "You're just as big a slob as your father." Similarity does not mean identical, we are all individuals. There may be hereditary similarities, that is, like father, like son or like mother, like daughter. Therefore, we react according to a formula. Because things may be similar, that does not mean they are identical. When we assume they are, our bias distorts our communication.

Sometimes we assume that change just cannot take place. This is drawing the wrong conclusion from the right facts - "You've always been that way; therefore, you'll always be that way." Then when the person does try to change, we immediately, and with great suspicion, consider his efforts as phony, unreal, and insincere - an attempt to get something in return. ("Thanks for the roses, dear; what have you done this time?") In marriage counseling this is known as an attempt to maintain the equilibrium or homeostasis within the relationship; that is, balance. That is seen when someone goes on a diet or makes other changes only to be sabotaged by their partner, usually unconsciously. It is precisely when you go on a diet that they want to take you out for pizza! Change is a frightening thing for many people. They resist it because they don't understand what the differences may mean or how their spouse or friend may be when changes do occur. Because of this, people prefer that change not take place at all. "I don't like the way you are, but I've had to live with it so long that I've gotten used to it. I'd rather live like that than with a stranger." This is especially evident with alcohol and drug abuse problems, sexual and other types of abuse within a dysfunctional family system - people would rather stay with what is known than the unknown. Becoming stuck in dysfunctional relationships is the result. What this person is really saying is, "I've learned to cope with you the way you are, and if you change, that means I'll have to change too. I don't want to change any more than you do, and I am not sure I can."[13]

Another area of difficulty can be contending with the subjective vs. the objective view of things. Things look different to me, subjectively - looking from my inside out than to you, subjectively, looking from your inside out. That's why we have differing accounts from eyewitnesses at trials or at the scene of an accident. I can not see things exactly the way you do, and if I don't make the effort, an issue may become unclear and fuzzy; we suffer from "communication astigmatism."

Still another problem can be caused by a lack of trust. A statement can be, "You failed me so often, I don't feel I can trust you any more." This is natural; we instinctively withdraw from pain. Contrary to the old joke, we don't keep hitting ourselves in the head with a hammer because it

---

[13] More on this in the section on "Counseling the Troubled Family."

feels so good when we stop! We become unwilling to risk ourselves with the other person on any level, which would put us in a trusting, and therefore vulnerable, position with them.

A further distortion to communication can be expecting perfection of ourselves and others. As one author puts it, "The only person who has the right to expect perfection of other people is the person who is perfect himself - and I don't know anyone like that!"

A final distortion can be a difference in educational levels and cultural differences. In these cases, the person with the greater education needs to help the one with the lesser education to have experiences which further deepen and broaden their learning. Furthermore, where there are differences in culture or heritage, an all-out effort to appreciate one another and gain a new outlook on where the other person is coming from and their differences is paramount.

None of these distortions are insurmountable but are certainly areas that we need to be aware of as Christians living in family relationship.

IMPROVING COMMUNICATION

Often the solution to a problem begins with a proper definition. The word "communication" comes from a Latin word meaning "to make common." Communication may be understood as a process through which ideas are transmitted among people by use of a common language. Our earliest use of communication is in calling other people to our needs, such as a babies cry. There are at least six versions of every spoken communication. They are:

- What the speaker intended to say.
- What the speaker actually said.
- What the speaker thought he said.
- What the listener wanted to hear.
- What the listener actually heard.
- What the listener thought he heard.
So what can we then do to improve communication? First, let me outline the simple method of effective communication, and then we will explore how to improve communication.

SIMPLE COMMUNICATION MODEL

When one person is ready to communicate to another, whether verbal, non-verbal, or symbolic, first the initiator of the communication determines within their own mind a message that is going to be sent...then they choose the method of sending the message. For sake of illustration, let's assume that the communication is verbal. One person is going to make a statement to another person. When they make their statement, or even before they do, he or she makes the statement or communication it will naturally be filled with specific biases caused by their perceptions, belief systems, history, self-image, and their belief about the other person's care or concern for them. All of biases or perceptions go into the making up of this message. When they speak, the person that is giving the message assumes clarity and understandability. According to the diagram to follow, this message goes directly to the other person and is received by them. As it is received, the person interprets the meaning of the message based upon their belief system, history, perception of the situation, etc. Not always is the message interpreted exactly as it is sent because of the receiving individual's perceptual distortions, or what is commonly called "noise." So, simply put, a message is not clearly understood unless both people hear it the same way it was sent.

In order to determine clarity, a person must ask for feedback. Feedback helps to insure that the message sent is the message received. An example might help illustrate. I say to my friend, "Gee, that's an interesting shirt that you're wearing." My friend responds, "Well, if you don't like it, stick it in your ear." Apparently my friend has heard a message from me that says, "I don't like the shirt", When in reality I do.

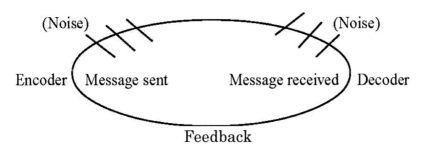

The way to deal with that is either defensively or, hopefully if I am a good communicator, I would ask for feedback. "Gee, what did you hear me say by my message?" He might respond, "You don't like my shirt." "Oh no, that's not what I meant. I like your shirt; I think it's very nice." At that point, we are both clear about the meaning of my message. We have both interpreted it the same. Without feedback, we can have fights, distortions, or misinterpretations which lead to conflict in relationship. This model is very simple, but hopefully it will help you understand the basic dynamics of communication. One key to effective communication is seeking feedback ("What I heard you say is"...) to ensure communication is clearly understood.

Moving on, what can we do then to improve our communication with one another as couples and within the family? First and foremost we must have a desire to improve our communication. Remember, communication is not a one-way street. Both parties must want to improve it. If one is trying and the other is not, it can be difficult and frustrating. If both say, "We haven't been communicating as we ought, let's try," then there is great hope.

First, it is important to learn to listen to one another. Jesus was a master at listening to the needs of his disciples and people in general. He was quick to listen and slow to speak. Listen actively and emphatically. Watch the other person's inflection, body language, and facial expressions. Try to ascertain the "feeling tone" or listen to the "music," the feelings, not just the words. This type of listening takes practice. The separation between broadcast bands on a radio dial is so narrow that they are easily missed. If you do miss, you're tuned in on the wrong wave-length and getting the wrong signals. We have to learn to pick up the signals, otherwise, no matter what the other person says to you, he is talking to himself. This is a monologue, not a dialogue.

Make a study of the other person's vocabulary. Learn to speak the other person's language rather than assuming that you have the only right way of speaking. Think, for example, how different the teenager's definition of "square" is from that of the older generation.

Further, it is important to recognize the basic sex and personality differences between men and women. For instance, many counselors find that women are far more troubled by anxiety than men. They also find that men have greater difficulty with pride and self-centeredness. Pastors and their wives can struggle with the difference between church and home. God's man of Faith and power, especially seen within Pentecostal circles must be compared with God's Men having "sore feet" and "bad breath," etc. It is important to recognize the differences between men and women and learn to adapt to differing communication styles and needs as we learn to love one another.

There certainly are gender differences. Specifically, a person's non-biased existence is limited to a few minutes immediately following birth before his/ her sex is announced to his parents. As soon as his/her sex is announced, a whole set of preconceived roles are superimposed upon the newborn. These roles can affect the clothing that the child will wear in the future, the types of games the child may play, it may affect how the child will be allowed to cope with his/her emotions. For instance, little girls are allowed to show their feelings more demonstratively, whereas "big boys don't cry."

Furthermore, the child's comfort with sexuality will become quite evident. Parental fears of premarital pregnancy with all of its concomitants prompt much more severe discipline for sexually curious girls than boys. Boys are frequently allowed a little more comfort with their sexuality. In fact, in many cases fathers encourage a certain amount of "boys will be boys." Wise parents gradually introduce positive person-centered reasons for premarital chastity, that is, the need to center a relationship in love and respect. Sexual desire reaches its peak for men between 20 and 28, although certainly they are not limited sexually beyond that age. Women seem to reach their peak in their early thirties. These differences need to be remembered as we talk about family life and communication.

Continuing on, by late adolescence, internalized cultural expectations have broadened the disparity between masculine and feminine world views. Women seem to demonstrate a bit more social intelligence than men do. Men feel a much greater urgency to "succeed," especially in areas of career than women do although this has been changing due to the women's liberation movement experienced over the last few decades.

In some ways, men have more freedom than women. They have a certain relative freedom of movement and are less subject social restrictions. In other ways women have more freedom than men do. They seem to have more freedom of emotional expression amongst peers, as well as across the sexes, and freedom to express feeling towards members of the same sex.

Upon entering marriage, having different world views, men and women bring with them very different needs and expectations. When large groups of women are asked what they want most in a husband, they might say someone to be kind and understanding with them, a romantically affectionate husband, a good father for their children, or a good provider. When large groups of men are asked the same question in regards to spousal attributes, they would say a reasonably good housekeeper, a reasonably good cook, an interesting and exciting sex partner, and a good mother for their children.

We don't really have an answer to the differences in regards to how to bridge the gap in communication other than to recognize that these differences between masculine and feminine worlds remain to be bridged by communication and understanding. It is important that we remember ways men and women are alike as well as how they are different.

Of significant note is that there is no measurable difference between men and women in regards to intelligence. However, both have sensitive egos; each seeks to enhance their life and to defend against hurt. Both men and women appreciate respect and resent being used. Both need sufficient freedom for self fulfillment. A mature wife will help her husband enjoy expressing the erotic side of his nature. A mature husband will help his wife enjoy expressing the erotic side of her nature. It is important to remember that both men and women were created by God, different but equal, to be complementary, not competitive. Each is incomplete in him or herself but fulfilled (potentially) in each other.

Learn to catch the bridges, to recognize when the other person is building a communication bridge toward you. The husband says, "Would you like to go out for dinner?" The wife responds, "I don't care." The husband says, "I really want to bless you, where would you like to go!" the wife, "It doesn't matter. You decide." The husband says, "Oh, forget it. I didn't want to go out anyhow," and on it goes.

Now each was saying something good and legitimate. The husband "I love you, I'm proud of you. You've been working hard and I'd like to give you a break by treating you to dinner." The wife, "I love you. I'm grateful to you, but I know how tight the budget has been. Though I would love to go out with you I do not know what you can afford. I do not want to go overboard. You pick a place you can handle; any place is all right with me."

Because neither understood the principle of bridge-building, the whole bridge went "plop" into the river. This needless interchange will occur unless we are aware of bridges of human communication and how people use them, and to use feedback when communication seems confused.

It is helpful to recognize the other person's coping patterns. There are three basic coping patterns. The first is **flight**; "Let me out of here. I can't deal with what is going on so I want to run away." The second is **fight**; "Get out of the way or I will mow you down! I'll show you how powerful I am, I'll huff and I'll puff and I'll blow your house down." The third and certainly the most functional is to **face and solve**. "Come, let us reason together, and let us work out this problem, with the help of the Lord." Each can be an adequate defense at times, depending on the situation. We need to learn to be versatile, to use them all, but not one to the exclusion of the rest; that can cause great problems in our relationships.

LOVE IS SUPREME

All people must learn to love. Love should be learned first, the natural way, from mother's breast. If it is not learned there, it becomes increasingly harder year by year to learn. But it can be learned by following William James' principle of habit formation. That is, **first**, begin as soon as possible. **Second**, repeat the effort as often as possible. **Third** allow as few exceptions as possible and look for the good! You've got to "accentuate the positive and eliminate the negative."

If motivated by love, couples can work towards effective and healthy communication.

The final skill needed is a stronger spiritual life for the couple and the family. Two people of the same mind and spirit will have a far better chance of establishing good communication, on a far higher and deeper plain, than a pair who is at odds over basic spiritual principles. Amos 3:3 states, "Can two walk together, except they be agreed?" Can they indeed?

The best advice for a couple who want to learn good communication comes from Paul the apostle:

> "Let this mind be in you which was also in Christ Jesus..."

All of this is predicated on a healthy sense of self. We all need assistance at times in this area, but if an individual is very weak in ego (that is, without sound counseling and self-insight), there will be consistent problems. The Holy Spirit will help us...if we allow Him to.

COMMUNICATION IN MARRIAGE

As already indicated, communication is vitally important to healthy human relationships. This, of course, is especially true in marriage Let us define what communication in marriage is all about. The first definition is by H. Brandt who says, "Communication means to overcome the desire to conceal feelings and thoughts, and to rise to the level of honesty about money, fears, wishes, motivations, sex feelings and responses, mistakes made, resentments and misunderstandings." J. Ruesch states, "That human function which people use to relate to each other. By means of signals and signs, human beings exchange views, express inner thoughts and feelings, make agreements and state disagreements." H. Robinson says, it's "a meeting of meanings."

Within the Word of God here is much said about communication. The basis of communication in marriage is found in Ephesians 4:14-15 (NIV):

> "Then we will be no longer infants, tossed back and forth by the waves, and blown here and there by every wind of teaching and by the cunning and craftiness of men in their deceitful scheming. Instead, speaking the truth in love, we will in all things grow up into Him who is the Head, that is, Christ."

"The heart of marriage is its communication system. The problems and potential of that communication system touch every couple. It can be said that the success and happiness of any married pair is measurable in terms of the deepening dialogue which characterizes their union. For this reason, our task is to understand what communication involves, both as verbal and nonverbal interaction, and how it applies to the intimate nature of marriage." (Small, p. 11).

Furthermore, Bourdeau states that "Without communication, there can be no adjustment at all. Ability to converse on any subject is the bedrock of marriage. It isn't always verbal. Attitudes are expressed by a smile, a frown, a shrug. These are powerful. We sense disapproval even though the spoken words are reassuring."

Small again writes, "What an exciting and meaningful discovery it is to lose one's sense of separateness and aloneness in the thrill of a close identification with another; it is exhilarating."

Open and loving communication in marriage is vital. Listed here are five levels of communication, in descending order, from five to one. You may be able to identify where you are in regards to your communication with your spouse within your marriage.

Level 5 is the cliché, conversation level of communication. That is, really no communication at all. There is no sharing of persons. The conversation involves around the club-house, Laundromat, etc. It's a "Hello. How are you today?" "Fine, thank you. How are you!?" form of communication.

Level 4 is reporting the facts about others. It is a form of communication that reveals almost nothing about ourselves. It just reports facts, no comment on them, just facts and figures. Like, "I went to the store today." "I went to work and came home." "The weather was nice."

Level 3 begins to become more intimate. It consists of the **sharing of ideas and judgments** to another person. This is an attempt at communication of who I am inside. It tells you some of my ideas and reveals some of my judgments. If you don't accept my ideas and judgments, however, I will probably retreat to safer ground.

Level 2 then moves one step deeper. It is called **gut level communications**. That is a level of communication where I tell you not only what is on my mind, but also how I feel.

Any relationship which is to have the nature of personal encounter must be based on this honest, open, gut-level communication. This is a risky level of communication with another, yet it is the only level that is truly genuine.

Level 1 is called **peak communication**.
This level of communication does that happens all the time; it really only happens rarely, and with perhaps a few in a lifetime. This level of communication has absolute openness and honesty. It is complete emotional and personal communion with another human being. In the author's book, The Journey to Wholeness, the concept of the need for an intimate relationship as being the first level of need for a young Christian is presented. Just as for a child coming into the natural world needs unconditional care, so do children of God. Yet in many ways, this level of absolute vulnerability in relationship is just for a few, for God being one and primary. This level of communion with a spouse or other significant person can be life transforming, and something to pray for.

BACK TO THE GUT

Let's look at guidelines for "gut-level" communication, since this is the area of greatest importance. Gut-level communication, that is communication with open emotions and honesty, does not allow for judgment of the other person. You see, emotions are neither good nor bad. They are neither moral nor immoral. In fact, feelings and emotions must be integrated with the intellect and the will. In gut-level communication emotions must be reported or stated to the other person in such a way as they understand the meaning of your words. With rare exceptions, emotions must be reported at the time they are experienced, not at some later date. One problem seen in marriages occurs when one person is hurt by a message they have heard but they do not share those feelings until some time later. That is not a productive form of communication, except in a case of extreme anger, where it may be important to hold in feelings for a while, and then express them in a more productive way.

Again, in review, there are many potential problems in communication. These problems include listening and silence, disagreements and attacks against the person, competition between people, and an inability to forgive one another for actual or perceived past hurts. When there is a myth of perfection, that is where one person assumes perfection in self while the other one is flawed, communication can be nearly impossible. Of course, only God is perfect, and the myth is just that. In spite of potential problems, positive communication is possible and obtainable, but like a beautiful garden must be cultivated and cared for.

Cultivating Positive Communication

How can we cultivate positive communication between husbands and wives?

Husbands can show affection to their wife at least daily. Give her a hug and a kiss unexpectedly, not just the perfunctory kiss in the morning on the way out the door, and the pat on the head (while you kiss the dog) when you come in at night. Rather, an unsolicited hug or kiss that shows that you really care about your spouse has meaning. Do not underestimate the value and meaning of small, seemingly insignificant and inexpensive gifts. One of the most precious things that a husband can do is to write his wife a small love letter, a poem, or give her a small gift that expresses gratitude for her. Remember men, tenderness is not equated with weakness. Jesus was tender toward all people, yet he certainly was not weak.

It is important to kiss your wife in public once in a while. Do not be afraid to hold her hand and give her a hug in front of others. It is a statement to your wife that she is special not just to you, but that you want the rest of the world to know how special she is. Give her a phone call from work just to say hello, even when you do not have to. Tell her that you love her. It is important to use good manners at all times, especially in public with your wife. Do not use your wife as the focus of jokes, but instead be protective of her, not because she is weaker but to show respect. These are just a few of the many things that husbands can do; there are others that revolve around the issue of being kind, considerate, and loving towards your spouse and showing it in ways that are practical for her.

For wives, little things can be done to show that you care for your husband, such as wearing perfume even if you are not going out. Many husbands just love to know that their wives smell good; they like to be around her. Avoid being a pin curl and cold-cream wife. Be attractively feminine, the best you can be. The key to doing so is motivation. Many times women say, "But you do not understand. If my husband would..." Don't worry about what he does; the key is to be motivated to look your best. Be positive about your husband, especially in public. You do not need to lie or exaggerate, but it is important that you be positive and show respect for him, especially in the public arena. This will cover a multitude of sins.

For husbands and wives it is important to develop special covenants or agreements with one another, especially regarding public behavior. An example from a friend's marriage might help. When they would attend social gatherings, whether at church or office, especially where the main friends were the husband's, the wife would frequently feel insecure. The husband's style was very social, flitting from one person to another, enjoying socializing with others without awareness of his wife's sense of insecurity. The wife shared her uncomfortable feelings with her husband, who's most appropriate response was to ask how to remedy the situation for her. They developed a little signal with one another. The signal was nothing more than a look that indicated they needed to reconnect and show more closeness to overcome the uncomfortable feelings. These covenants or signals, if developed, can help relationships, as they indicate that the marriage is primary over other relationships.

Things that can help build communication and strengthen the marriage for both husband and wife include taking a walk in the rain, or in the sunshine for that matter, together. Don't forget to hold hands. Spend a night in a retreat center, together and away from the kids, a special time for the two of you. Building each other up in public cannot be overemphasized. Go out regularly, not you and another couple, but just the two of you, for a chance to share feelings. Never say, "It seems to me a good wife (or a good husband) would..." Instead, if you focus with thankfulness that this is the husband or wife that God has allowed you to find, and you focus on the positive, God will bless you as you build up one another.

GOD'S PERSPECTIVE

"Long ago God spoke in many different ways to our fathers through the prophets (in visions, dreams, and even face to face), telling them little by little about His plans. But now in these days He has spoken to us through His Son to whom He has given everything and through whom He made the world and everything there is (Hebrews 1:1-2 in the Living Bible).

Communication is the lifeline of relationships. The health of any relationship is determined by the quality of communication between or among the people involved.

These observations underscore a truth as old as the Garden of Eden and as real as Calvary. Man's relationships with God was so damaged that it took centuries of patient persistence by God to re-establish them.

If it taxed the patience and creativity of God to finally break through man's communication barrier with His love, don't be disheartened if one has trouble getting his message through to someone he loves. Admittedly, good communications can be painstaking and difficult; but healthy, happy relationships are their reward.

THE DEVELOPMENT OF COMMUNICATION

Man was born with a built-in way of calling attention to his needs...crying. For the first six months of an infant's life, the infant's cry essentially rules his/ her world. About the time that the child begins to cry, the father wants a little more attention from mother so he opines, "Honey, if you don't quit running every time that kid cries, you are going to spoil him rotten." This statement can appear to be motivated by love and concern for the child, but in many cases it is motivated from the need of the husband for special attention. Eventually the baby learns that crying won't work to get her/his needs met, they move to the next stage of cry... temper tantrums. Temper tantrums become a new way that a child brings others to his/her needs (sometimes you feel it will bring you to your knees!). Temper tantrums are relatively normal for pre-school children, as long as they are not constant. Most parents discover ways of extinguishing this behavior once the child learns to talk. If children are still throwing temper tantrums after they have begun school, they have usually been ignored or indulged by their parents.

By age four, a child becomes aware of psychological needs for which his young vocabulary is still inadequate. Thus he calls attention to himself by the display of various moods. Moods are often expressed by love tests. Such tests may include the constant pulling on momma's dress, the asking of questions over and over, requesting to play the same game over and over again. Where possible, reasonable parental efforts should be made to meet the child's love tests. It is important not to discourage a child early in life while at the same time recognizing the difference between manipulative behavior, attention seeking behavior on the child's part and genuine need for parental contact.

By seven years of age, a child has developed a sizable abstract vocabulary which he often uses to get his way by nagging. This can be a very difficult time for parents. It is important to learn to listen to the music of what a child is saying, and not just the words. Learning to respond positively where possible while selectively ignoring negative nagging behavior is a key to communication at this stage of development.

During the **middle teens,** when dating behavior becomes prominent, young people have developed elaborate systems of rational thinking. Many are anticipating marriage. Because of that, youth often have difficulty accepting some of their parent's irrational communication as part of normal family life. Frequently they insist that disagreements among them and their eventual families will be settled by reasonable discussion. We oftentimes ask, "Why doesn't it turn out that way?" The reasons for that seem to be fairly evident - each person has his/her own frustration tolerance. When this tolerance is exceeded, the person is likely to regress (that is, go back to) a level of irrational communication that worked reasonably well for him as he was growing up. This can be seen with new couples, when the husband doesn't seem to get what he wants, he will throw a temper tantrum or punch a hole in the wall as an expression of his frustration. To help minimize these uncomfortable, awkward times in the home, a family may explore other approaches to communication, which are significantly healthier and more productive.

DIFFERENT APPROACHES TO COMMUNICATION

More positive and healthy ways to communicate to others can include:

- The acceptance of another's behavior whenever possible, and without judgment.
- Become a good listener. Again, not only listening to the words, but to the meaning of the words, or to the "music" of a person's expression.

- Learn to respond to the needs of others with respect, and provide loving responses where possible.
- When you must fight, follow the rules discussed in the next section.

In conclusion, family communications are a vital part of family life. Being in communion with Christ can help families establish good communications with each other. A conscious effort on each member's part will make it easier for the whole family to "live together and even like it!"

"There's a reason God made you with two ears and one mouth...so you can listen twice as much as you talk!"
Carma Louise DeKoven

CONFLICTS AND THEIR RESOLUTIONS

The attempt has been made to concentrate on the positive aspects of family life and to teach basic principles which will keep the family happy through the life cycle. Yet, recognition must be made that there can be unresolved conflicts in any family. These unresolved conflicts, if not dealt with properly, can disrupt healthy family living. A result of unresolved conflict can be seen in what is called "dirty fighting." There are several forms of dirty fighting that can occur. Provided here are certain titles and that will assist in understanding areas of conflict and provide strategies for intervention.

DIRTY FIGHTING

The first one is **THE SPY**. The spy is the individual within the family which gathers information (negative) for future use. They are looking, searching their environment for any cue that would validate that their belief that their partner could do something to hurt them. The spy is suspicious, cannot trust, and can cause great problems within a family relationship. Another dirty fighting technique is...

THE SHOTGUN METHOD. That is, one partner will blast all of their anger and hurt on friends and family without recognizing who is really at fault in a given situation. Rather than being specific, they will blow in a random pattern against anyone who happens to walk in their path at the time. Often the blast is a defensive response to being "caught" and sends a message that one would be best off not confronting them for self-preservation. Another form of dirty fighting is...

THE TEASE. The tease is someone who is passive-aggressive in their style, or subtle in anger. They may use sarcastic humor, or other forms of angry comments that mask their feelings or intentions. They rarely state how they really feel to avoid being responsible for their feelings or actions. The next is...

LABELS. They will use certain names or labels to characterize or categorize an individual within the relationship. Such labels as paranoid, dependent, inadequate, stupid - all which tend to project blame and an image of superiority, while accusing the other person of being less of a human being. These labels can stick after awhile and can become very painful. Another next form of dirty fighting is to...

IGNORE YOUR SPOUSE. An example of this would be is a man or woman initiates an argument or discussion, the partner walks away, changes the subject, or just refuses to talk about it. This has two main advantages. First, it generally drives the spouse right up the wall, increasing anger and frustration, because the message usually perceived is: "You're not even worth arguing with." Second, this tactic enables the person to feel superior and rationalize their behavior with statements like: "When you calm down and act like an adult, I'll talk about it" or, "When you're ready to discuss it rationally, let me know." Ultimately, the one doing the ignoring has the power, and is usually using this technique to control and/or to punish. Another form of dirty fighting would be that of...

BEING CONDESCENDING. "Giving in" for the sake of the children can be a form of condescension. This is a beautiful way to turn the tables on one's spouse, especially when you know you are wrong and are losing the battle. This helps insure one's feeling of superiority and provides a sort of moral victory in the face of defeat. Such apparent surrender is not humiliating, since it can be considered a tactical retreat with a view to future combat and ultimate victory. This is a form of false humility and spiritual pride. Another dirty fighting tactic, which that often occurs in familes is the...

INSISTENCE ON JUSTICE. Or, perhaps more accurately put, you want to get your pound of flesh! If you feel you have been wronged, it is important to balance the scales or take revenge. Emphasize your own rights, and ignore those of your partner. This will make it easier for you to justify the "just punishment" you mete out. This can be accomplished in apparently innocent yet very effective ways. For example, you start suffering headaches or developing ills to avoid sexual relations. You might overspend, thus throwing a wrench into a carefully planned budget. If you prefer, you can always act like a martyr. One more form, which seems somewhat subtle, is the stance of...

BEING OPEN AND FRANK AT ALL TIMES. They think, "Whatever you do, do not suppress your feelings or limit your expression of opinions, views, and the like." If you do not like your wife's hairdo, a meal, a personal habit, get it out, communicate; be frank. These are excellent ways to hurt and maim while justifying yourself by appealing to the need for open and frank communication in marriage. Speaking the truth at all costs (void of love or sensitivity) costs too much.

BE A CHRONIC FORGETTER is the next category. Constantly make promises and offer to help your spouse, but be sure to let your partner down by forgetting. The value of this technique lies in the fact that you can be very hostile and punishing (passive/aggressive), and still protect yourself by claiming human weakness and fallibility. Another area is...

BE TOO HELPFUL. Seek out your spouse's shortcomings. Be on the alert for mistakes and failings so that you can offer help and advice. They generally believe that their spouse is a reflection of themselves and thus have the right to remake their spouse into a suitable reflection of themselves. This spouse thinks it is their duty to help their spouse improve. Being overly helpful can easily undermine their spouse's sense of individuality and self-worth, and can even have the advantage of making them feel guilty that he/she is not a better mate for them.

These last two are probably the two most important categories, and the most damaging.

USE THE CHILDREN AS WEAPONS. When it comes to dirty fighting, parents have a distinct advantage. They will use every weapon if they feel attached. For example, they contradict their spouse's authority with the children, especially in his/her absence. They make the children aware of their spouse's shortcomings; not missing a chance to compare him or her unfavorably with others within the hearing of the children. They may pick fights with him/her in front of the children; attack their spouse's behavior toward the children when something else is really the issue. It is very apparent how destructive this can be within a marital relationship, and is tremendously detrimental to the healthy growth of the children. One form of this unfair fighting technique is triangulation, where a child is used in the middle of parents' communication. This gives the child way too much power, and can cause significant wounding to all involved. Finally...

USE SEXUALITY AS A WEAPON. Since this is probably the most intimate and vulnerable part of a relationship, they are sure to attack their mate's masculinity or femininity, not overlooking the maiming potential of subtle comparisons. Suggesting that one is abnormal, frigid, oversexed, and the like is a powerful weapon. Faking headaches or illness, developing an abundant supply of excuses to use in avoiding sexual intimacy with a view to improving a bargaining position can be used. Playing games with each other, which may include flirting, teasing, or sending double messages (I want you, just not tonight) are powerfully painful weapons. To stimulate and then reject and refuse are frequent parts of this destructive play. So what can be done if these types of destructive and hurtful communication styles are a part of a couple's repertoire? Well, after repentance and seeking forgiveness, one might try these.

- **Stick to the subject**. When a couple looks back at a fight they may have had, they recognize that they often started out on one topic and ended up in something entirely different, usually bringing up old hurts from the past. Rehearsing the past and getting off subject is not an effective way to deal with issues and problems in a relationship.

- **Don't fight dirty**. We call those in counseling terminology "belt line" issues. You just don't want to hit below the belt. It is important that you learn those sensitive areas that your partner has and be careful not to hit below the belt. That can cause long term damage to a relationship.

- **Learn to make reasonable adjustments** toward your partner. That means to learn to look through the other person's eyes instead of just through your own.

- **Look back on your fights with good humor and learn** from them. Recognize destructive patterns and try to change them. It is important to control your anger and emotional expression.

RESOLUTION OF ANGER

It is inevitable that one will become angry at times. This is especially true within families. Many of the problems in marriage occur due to the lack of recognition of the feelings of anger, nor the ability to express and resolve anger effectively.

People do not want to admit feelings of anger. Christians particularly feel guilty about having angry feelings, especially against a family member or a brother and sister in Christ. Beyond this, few have been taught how to handle angry feelings in a controlled, restrained way, while effectively communicating angry and other feelings in an appropriate manner.

Webster defines anger as "an affliction, a strong feeling of displeasure." Synonyms for anger are ire, rage, fury, resentment, indignation, and wrath. Psychological anger is a human emotion; it is energy, a drive or impulse. We feel it as a feeling of displeasure, irritation, or frustration. It is essentially a biological response to hurt, rejection or an obstacle in the fulfillment of one's desire.

How do we recognize anger? It is painful to recognize and admit that we have a problem with anger. Because **Christians feel guilty about anger**, they may rephrase their responses saying they are "hurt." Others will rephrase it as being "disappointed," "frustrated," or "disturbed." Other forms of anger include repressed emotion or silence, which may lead to depression or psychosomatic illness. Some even deny the presence of anger, even though it may be apparent to others. There is a great need for honesty here. This is the first step in resolving anger, which can build bridges to communication rather than walls of opposition.

What does the Word of God say about anger? Let's look at a few scriptures. For reference you might refer to the following scriptures. (Proverbs 14:17, 29; 16:32; 19:11; Ecclesiastics 7:9; James 1:19; and Mark 3:5.) A common theme from the above scriptures is restraint and self-control. Therefore, it is not having the feeling of anger that is sin, but what we do with it that matters. When anger becomes wrath, when we attack or say foolish things to hurt, this is sinful (James 3:14-18; Eph. 4:22-32). The answer to sin is confession that leads to repentance, restitution, reconciliation and restoration.

An angry, hostile reaction is destructive, as it often comes n a form of an attack. When we attack, we attempt to denigrate or destroy the character of a person. We attack the person rather than the act, and in doing so we defend our hurt and avoid hearing the person we attack. Communication is difficult and anger often goes underground and unresolved (Heb. 12:14-15).

Therefore, to change this reaction, we must learn to respond appropriately (Eph. 4:26). Our feelings must be identified, named or labeled accurately for what they are. As we claim or acknowledge our feelings, (that is, to make the statement "it is my feeling,") we take a step towards personal responsibility for them and move one step closer to handling them appropriately.

Anger must be expressed in a controlled, appropriate fashion. If expressed without harm, explosion or over-reaction, but rather to help to ourselves and others, our expressions of anger can be beneficial. Therefore, when we express angry feelings in appropriate ways to benefit others, especially our spouse or children, it leads to healthy relationship. We do this best by learning assertiveness, expressing our feelings in a **confrontation, yet without condemnation**. To be assertive is to make a statement, "I recognize that you are a person of worth. I recognize that you have a position of authority, and I am upset about a certain thing that was said or done." First acknowledge the individual's position, showing respect for them as a creation of God, and yet at the same time we acknowledge that people can make mistakes or cause harm. Within God's word are examples of healthy interchanges, which lead to healthy outcomes.

For example, Paul and Peter had conflicts. Peter, who at one point had been living a life without prejudice became prejudice against the Greeks and for the Jews. The Word of God says that Paul confronted him to his face about his error. Peter, recognizing his error, repented. That is the appropriate way to deal with anger between people. Our goal is to seek **repentance, restitution, reconciliation** and **restoration** in all relationships. That is the main meaning behind not letting the sun go down on our wrath and therefore giving place to the devil. (Eph. 4:26) We need to deal with our anger when we feel it, and never give the devil a chance to come between us and the people that we love.

Section III

Special Concerns In The Family

"The way out of trouble is never as simple as the way in."
Ed Howe

SECTION III

INTRODUCTION

There are many concerns that families will have, challenges they will face which are, in many ways, unique to our common era. Not every possible concern could be adequately discussed in one volume, but key special concerns of family life are presented here. As with what has been written previous to this section, the prevention of problems is the focus.

SELF-IMAGE:

DEVELOPING A CHRIST-LIKE SELF-CONCEPT

It is said that we live in the age of narcissism or self-centeredness. So many people are trying to find out, "Who am I? Where do I fit?" There seems to be an obsession with trying to build oneself up, to overcome victimization, etc. As Christians, the focus on self is not to develop a positive self-image, which often leads to self-deception. However, the development of a godly self-concept rooted in Christ is essential to our peace, happiness and productivity.

What is self-image? Simply stated, it is how one thinks and feels about oneself: his/her intellectual abilities, his/her physical appearance (height, weight, shape, hair, facial features, etc.), his/her personality (style of relating to others), his/her talents. There are several characteristics of a poor self-image. They include:

- One who finds it difficult accepting compliments from others.

- One who cannot easily share oneself to form close friendships. They tend to be social isolates to keep themselves from being hurt. Another characteristic of a person with poor self-image is a person
- One who downgrades themselves on a regular basis. Furthermore...
- One who accepts constructive criticism personally and gets depressed and angry about it is indicative of someone who has a poor image of self. Also,
- One who accepts inaccurate criticism as true and begins to believe it is showing signs of a poor self-image. Finally,
- One who holds on to past failures and consciously or unconsciously punishes himself for those failures is lacking in Christ-like self worth.

What are some of the characteristics of a good self-image? Someone with a good self-image is...

- One who enjoys all of his abilities and seeks to cultivate his expertise in them. It is also...
- One who is able to spot another's poor self-image and looks for ways to help, when possible, without attempting to rescue them. It is also...
- One who sees his/her unique contribution to fellow Christians and seeks to share his gifts with them, not as a way of boasting, but in order to show love and kindness to others. A person with a good self-image is...
- One who is able to accept compliments from others. Furthermore...
- One who enjoys close friendships and is not afraid to risk relationships with others. Finally, it is

- One who accepts criticism as a challenge to improve but doesn't give in to condemnation.

Many of you may be saying, "Isn't self-image or self-esteem nothing more than pride and arrogance in the individual?" There is a difference between pride and loving who you are in Christ. First, let us look at what pride is all about. "Pride is characterized by an exaggerated desire to win the notice or praise of others, and the rigid taking of a superior position in which other's opinions are virtually never regarded as good as one's own. Humility is characterized by accurate self-appraisal, responsiveness to the opinions of others, and a willingness to give praise to others before claiming it for one's self" (Self Esteem, Craig W. Ellison, ed., p. 5).

The Scripture allows and even encourages the practice of loving who you are. Listed here are a number of Scriptures that will give you a clear understanding of who you are in Christ and the image you are to have in Him. These include: NAS

Hebrews 2:6-11, *but there is a place where someone has testified: "What man that you are mindful of him, the son of man that you care for him? You made him a little lower than the angels; you crowned him with glory and honor and put everything under his feet." In putting everything under him, God left nothing that is not subject to him. Yet at present we do not see everything subject to him. But we see Jesus, who was made a little lower than the angels, now crowned with glory and honor because he suffered death, so that by the grace of God he might taste death for everyone. In bringing many sons to glory, it was fitting that God, for whom and through whom everything exists, should make the author of their salvation perfect through suffering. Both the one who makes men holy and those who are made holy are of the same family. So Jesus is not ashamed to call them brothers.* Genesis 1:26-31, *Then God said, "Let us make man in our image, in our likeness, and let them rule over the fish of the sea and the birds of the air, over the livestock, over all the earth, and over all the creatures that move along the ground." So God created man in his own image, in the image of God he created him; male and female he created them. God blessed them and said to them, "Be fruitful and increase in number, fill the earth and subdue it. Rule over the fish of the sea and the birds of the air and over every living creature that moves on the ground." Then God said, "I give you every seed-bearing plant on the face of the whole earth and every tree that has fruit with seed in it. They will be yours for food. And to all the beasts of the earth and all the birds of the air and all the creatures that move on the ground—everything that has the breath of life in it—I give every green plant for food." And it was so. God saw all that he had made, and it was good. And there was evening, and there was morning the sixth day.*

John 15:15, *I no longer call you servants, because a servant does not know his master's business. Instead, I have called you friends, for everything that I learned from my Father I have made known to you.*

Romans 12:3, *For by the grace given to me I say to every one of you: Do not think of yourself more highly than you ought, but rather think of yourself with sober judgment, in accordance with the measure of faith God has given you.*

Galatians 6:3-4, *If anyone thinks he is something when he is nothing, he deceives himself. Each one should test his own actions. Then he can take pride in himself, without comparing himself to somebody else, for each one should carry his own load.*

Additional verses: Psalm 8:4-5, Mark 12:30-31, Ephesians 5:28-33.

The need for redemption for all of us indicates helplessness, not worthlessness! Remember that loving who you are is not a cover-up for arrogance. As Christians we need to recognize that Jesus did not come and die on the cross to obliterate ourselves or our ego, but instead came to redeem or restore ourselves back to right relationship with Him. That happens instantaneously from God's viewpoint when we accept Christ as our Savior and His blood cleanses us from all our sins. It is also a process whereby we put off the old nature, renew our mind, and put on the new self, which is made in righteousness and truth. Remember, God never made junk! We are not junk as people. We may be helpless without Christ, but we are not worthless! We are bought with a price, a great price, because we were worth so much to God the Father that He sent His Son, Jesus, to die for us!

DEVELOPING A HEALTHY AND GODLY SELF IMAGE

How is self-image developed? Our self-image, or the way we see ourselves or our basic personality structure is developed primarily through a combination of genetics (nature) and interpersonal relationships (nurture). It comes from how we feel others see us, especially significant others such as mother, father, siblings, grandmother, grandpa, significant teachers, pastors, etc.

A key to developing a positive, godly self-image is love! First, love has not been communicated if it hasn't been felt in the life and heart of the object loved. The lover must keep on loving, trying different ways to love, until he strikes a responsive chord. This is a challenge to all of us as parents who may have a resistant child. We are never to give up trying to reach them with our love, as it can make all the difference in the world in the development of self-esteem. Love should be without inhibition, rigidity, or restraint. One cannot truly love another without affection (Love Therapy, P. Morris, pp. 100-105).

Developing a positive godly self-image is one of the ways that you can enhance family life. Whether husbands and wives, or as Christian parents, as we love one another as Christ loved, and learn to we love our neighbor as we love ourselves, we grow in a godly self-image. Further, as we love our children in practical ways, providing to them the three primary ingredients that they need for growth (unconditional love, a certain dose of freedom, and clear discipline and guidelines), and as love is provided in a genuine and consistent way, we assist them in developing a positive, godly self-image, which makes all the difference in their ability to embrace life with courage.

A final thought will help. Love affirmed is love confirmed. When we affirm our spouse and children as special gifts from God, we confirm that they have worth to us and others. Affirmation is properly done through positing words and frequent positive touch. Even Jesus was affirmed by the Father, "This is my beloved son, in whom I am well pleased." (Lu. 3: 22)

DIVORCE

Divorce is a highly difficult event that occurs all too often within the lives of the members of the Body of Christ. It is beyond the scope of this book to dwell on the causes and extent of divorce. Ministry to the broken is discussed later in this work. (see section 4). That divorce may occur between two precious human beings that have experienced significant and troubling loss must be accepted as fact. Even though they may have divorced under wrong conditions, as members of the body of Christ we must be willing to reach out and minister to them in their time of need.

If anything can be said about divorce, it is that it should be avoided where humanly possible, except in cases of abuse from a spouse or towards children, or other Biblically allowed situations! We must remember that it was never God's intention that any of us get divorced, but He desires us to live a life of fulfillment with one another.

For those who believe that divorce might be required, some advice is offered. First, don't slide into divorce. Many couples, because of a lack of giving attention to one another have taken each other for granted and can slide into divorce. Apathy through lack of love and concern for one another can set the stage for unhappiness leading to divorce.

Secondly, don't get talked into divorce. When talking to friends and neighbors, especially non-Christians, if one shares concerns and hurts you have towards a spouse, they may be like Job's friends, talking you into cursing God and dying in regards to your marriage. Whatever you do, don't let them talk you into divorce. Don't get hustled into divorce by others who would say, "Oh man, the freedom is so wonderful, not being tied down to a spouse." Yes, there is a certain amount of freedom, but there are always consequences; it is not worth the consequences. Don't be seduced into divorce by another person, another man, another woman, or by any other person, including the devil, who would say, "It's okay. You can divorce because your spouse has so many problems, so many needs, and you deserve better." Don't be seduced into divorce.

Sometimes restlessness in middle-age or self-loathing, boredom and a sense of uselessness can cause someone to consider divorce as an option. Yet, divorce will not change any of those situations; it can only make them worse. Almost any problem that can occur within a marriage, except severe abuse or continued infidelity can be solved at home. Boredom and tension can be remedied. Not picking up his socks or burning the pot roast can all be resolved. Divorce should not be an option, except in extreme cases.

Divorce only solves unworkable marriages. But, if we read the Scriptures carefully, there can always be a solution to even the most seemingly unworkable marriage if we learn to yield ourselves totally to Christ and seek wise counsel.

Avoid divorce dialog. Don't make it a part of your conversation because it shatters dreams, assumptions, and memories. Make a covenant with each other that the one topic you will never discuss is divorce. Further, avoid deliberate ugliness. Then, one can be chivalrous and say, "Okay, if that's what you want, I'll give it to you." Don't try to hurt each other to force divorce to be considered. Don't let media "success stories" cause tension in your already stressful marriage. It's the world's standard to believe that divorce is the answer that will solve all needs. Remember, there is only one real difference between a divorce and a death. In a divorce the corpse is still walking around as a constant reminder of the good and the bad, of the hopeful and the hopeless. Do not choose divorce as an option but avoid it where possible and seek the Lord's guidance in the resolution of your problems. As you do so, God will bless you for it is His hope that all marriages be restored, complete and whole in Him as we submit our lives to Christ.

DATING CAN BE DANGEROUS:

FELLOWSHIP IS THE BETTER WAY

Why is it that problems of poor communication sometimes develop in dating? Dating can be one of the most difficult transition times for adolescents. It is important to remember that dating is a recent phenomenon of our Western culture. Most of us were ill prepared for dating when we went through it, and our teen-agers will be the same. So what are some of the problems of poor communication and why do they develop?

First of all, the person one is dating may put on a "front" or a mask to impress the other individual. We all try and put our best foot forward. There may furthermore be educational or intellectual differences which may be quite acute. The person may be fearful to open up and express him or herself for fear of making a mistake or being rejected. There may be a lack of trust between the sexes. Also, there may be little interests in common to get a relationship properly started. One person may attempt to dominate another and shyness may hinder communication.

Spiritual backgrounds may be so different that it is difficult to communicate effectively. A major problem may develop if one person gets too serious too soon, or only one person is serious while the other is hoping for a casual relationship or friendship. One or both in the relationship may not want to face problems that develop. They may not agree on viewpoints, or may not want to argue, so they avoid the issue. One person does not speak loudly enough for the other to hear. They may not be good listeners, lacking communication skills. Often times, especially with teenagers, a poor self-image may limit the ability to develop a healthy relationship.

All of these can be difficult and dating itself can be a frightening adventure. So what are some of the "danger signals" in dating that parents should be aware of? The couple may start taking each other for granted. There may be too much physical attachment and involvement between the two. Furthermore, the couple may be too young to begin dating. One of the individuals may not be a born again Christian. When dating becomes exclusive, couples may isolate themselves from other friends, intensifying their involvement. This may not be healthy for them or for their relationship with the Lord which may be diminished because they are too involved. As noted above, there may be poor communication between them. A person may be too critical of the one he/she is dating - lacking respect in the relationship. Standards that have long been agreed to, especially in regards to sexual chastity, may be lowered to please the other person, or out of fear that they may loose them. Arguments and quarreling may hinder personal growth. Therefore, it is strongly recommended that parents, churches, etc., emphasize fellowship to Christian teen-agers, not dating.

There are pressures placed on teen-agers from peers, school and other sources. It is important that they learn to develop positive relationships that are non stressful. As soon as a relationship becomes exclusive in nature, there develops the chance of hurt, as well as the possibility of inappropriate and unhealthy behavior. It is important to recognize that dating, if it does occur, should be first and foremost amongst fellow believers. Secondly, wherever possible, it should be friendship oriented without the possibility of becoming exclusive. Teens should have as many friends as manageable. Developing those friendships will last a great deal longer than having one exclusive relationship during the high school years.

Dating maybe an inevitable process, but it is important to continue to teach and guide teen-agers so that they fully understand the possible ramifications of an exclusive relationship. As a part of parental instruction, teach them to remember that God has a better way - that of finding the one woman or one man for a lifetime so that God can fulfill us through that relationship

PG REQUIRED

Parental guidance is necessary in the process of mate selection. Though in Western culture parents do not select mates as is done in other cultures, they should be intimately involved with their teen in evaluating a potential mate long before the process of finding one begins.

ABOUT SINGLES

There is nothing wrong with being single. It is important to take a Biblical approach to singleness, such as is seen in 1 Corinthians 7:1-9. For example, singles are not to be conformed to the attitudes and standards of the world system that invade Christian churches. The world says that if a person is single and over 25, there must be something wrong. The Bible affirms singleness as a viable option for those who desire it.

Many singles may be single for reasons of personal choice. Some are reasonably selective, choosing to wait for a God appointed spouse. Others may be called by God to long term singlehood. A single person should be treated with equal respect as a married one.

Further, it is important to involve singles in church activities. However, they should not be taken for granted, assuming that single means having nothing meaningful to do. The church can load singles down with many, sometimes meaningless responsibilities. A point to remember is that it may be God's will for a person to be single, or it may be God's will for them to be single NOW. Live today; God will take care of tomorrow. The present state is part of God's plan, not just preparation for what may come later.

As a single person, it is important to build a positive attitude...remember being single is not a disease. Singles need not apologize for being single. Well meaning parents should teach children in the home that singleness is an option; help them develop wholesome attitudes early in life. Positive parental attitudes will go a long way towards building right attitudes in children. Furthermore, sensitivity towards singles should be shown, especially in the church; avoid teasing, manipulating, joking, or cutting remarks about being single. This is especially germane for parents who have older single children. We must not manipulate or push them into marrying before they are ready, if they are ever ready. We are to accept our young adults as they are. It is important to break down barriers and false attitudes toward singleness held by some, such as mission boards, that refuse to consider single men or women for missions' service. Further, it is important to avoid segregation: divorced or single. What would Jesus have said if he saw us segregating societal widows, those who have been divorced, in the way that many churches do? It is important that a singles ministry in a church have a special identity, but also that the singles be included as part of the larger family of God; for they certainly are.

THE EXTENDED FAMILY

In Bible times families were viewed quite different than in our modern era. There was intense loyalty and identification with ones family, consisting usually of nuclear (immediate) family and extended family (Grandma's and Grandpa's, Uncles and Aunts, cousins, etc...) all of whom generally lived in close proximity to one another. They relied upon each other for economic viability, protection, mutual support and strength. The nuclear family is still viewed as primary, but the extended family in the natural and spiritual (Body of Christ) must be seen as important, deserving of respect and is to be included within the boundaries of our nuclear family life.

SENIOR CITIZENS AND THE FAMILY

Senior citizens in Old and New Testament times were treated with great respect and honor. Oh, how times have changed! Now we look forward to setting our folks out to pasture, often attempting to find ways to avoid responsibility for them in their later years. Let's look for a moment at some of the problems of the elderly and how we can minister to them, for they are vital parts of individual families, and the family of God.

As people grow older they become more fragile or vulnerable in many areas of life. They may be unable to care for themselves completely, and thereby have difficulty in living by themselves. Many senior citizens have limited financial resources and may suffer from feelings of loneliness or rejection; some may be starved for love. Seniors may have difficulty relating to others socially since they feel as if they are a "fifth wheel" in society. Many seniors have dietary problems, physical handicaps or generally poorer health and may consider themselves a burden to the family. Further, they may have spiritual problems that have not been resolved due to declining health. Many elder citizens have been highly productive for many years, having given themselves to family and society. But because they are less productive now, they are often rejected, abused, and neglected, when they deserve to be treated with respect. Elder abuse and neglect should never be tolerated within Christian circle.

What are some things that the church and family members can do to meet the needs of the elderly? First, we need to follow the scriptural admonition to care for the elderly and respect their personhood. Further, we need to provide a comfortable place for them to live, to make sure their basic financial and medical needs are met. This can be done by linking the church resources with those of appropriate social agencies. There is no need to reinvent the wheel - we must do our best to help the elderly within our community to live out their lives in fulfillment. We can do so in a variety of fashions. These may include visitation of them on a regular basis, especially if they are homebound or in a rest home. Remembering their special days - birthdays and anniversaries can bless them immensely. Taking senior on short trips and including them in family life is vitally important. Where necessary, the church and families within the church could provide transportation for the running of errands, buying of groceries, etc. It is important that we provide transportation for church activities.

I still remember in my earliest childhood days that the church women in their 60's and 70's were usually the most loving, gentle and open to share of themselves unwaveringly to help teach us the gospel. We need to remember them in their older age.

Other areas of help that the church or families within the church can give are to assist them with tasks that they cannot do for themselves. Such mundane and simple tasks such as maintenance and upkeep of property, mowing of lawns, raking of leaves, putting on storm windows can bless an elderly brother or sister in Christ. Helping them move from one location to another is another service we can provide. If they cannot come to church, we need to take church to them. Help them to make contact with social agencies and other organizations.

It is important that we do not get discouraged because of their discouragement. Many elders are somewhat disillusioned with where they are in life. We must motivate them to become all that God has created them to be in their later years, without becoming discouraged. The church can also help with financial matters if they are in a position to do so, but most assuredly the church can provide spiritual counsel and guidance from the Word of God.

Growing old is part of the family life cycle. It is not an unusual thing and does not have to be a frightening one. Western culture often attempts to avoid the very discussion of growing old, because of our fear of death and dying. The church should be involved in preparing individuals and families for retirement years and for issues related to end of life issues, early in adult years. This can best be done by including our grandparents and great-grandparents in family life, being there during their time of trouble; praying for them and caring for them in and through the church. It is not necessary for elders to grow bitter as they approach old age. They can grow better in deeper, wisdom and knowledge of the things of Christ, and remain productive until called home to be with the Lord.

We will all face the limitations of growing old and the inevitability of death. How we treat our elders will effect our eventual treatment, for you reap what you sow.

IN-LAW RELATIONSHIPS

There are many scriptures that provide a basis for appropriate in-law relations. There have been many jokes told about mother-in-laws and father-in-laws and how they sometimes meddle or become overly involved in a marriage. That certainly can happen, yet it does not have to. It behooves each family and married couple to be aware of the needs and specific issues in regards to in-laws and be ready to deal with them effectively.

In Exodus 22:23-24 the Word of God says, "Thou shalt not afflict any widow..." (NAS, all of these) Furthermore, in Deut. 14:28-29 it says that we are to "Provide for widows so that the Lord may bless thee." In Deut. 16:11 it says "Thou shalt rejoice (including widows) in the place the Lord has chose." "Widows may have the gleanings after the harvest" - Deut. 24:17 states. "The Lord relieveth the widow" Psalm 146:9. Furthermore, the Bible says "Do not oppress the widow" Jer. 7:6 and "Let thy widows trust in me" Jer. 49:11. In Mark 12:40, Matt. 23:14 and Luke 20:47 Jesus says, "Woe unto you scribes and Pharisees, for you devour widows' houses." Furthermore in Matt. 15:3-4 it says, "Honor parents - he who speaks evil of parents, let him be put to death." "The widows were neglected in daily ministration...select from among you, brethren, seven men of good reputation...whom we put in charge of this task...service of food)" in Acts 6:1. It is important that we "honor widows that are widows indeed...provide for them" as stated in 1 Tim. 5:3-16. "Pure religion and undefiled before God is this...to visit the widows in their distress..." James 1:27. There are also several passages in the Old Testament that also include the stranger and the fatherless. We must remember that in any possible in-law situation it is important to respect and show honor to them as discussed in the Word of God.

What are some specific problems which may develop in in-law relationships? One of the biggest problems, already noted above, is interference from in-laws. Sometimes they will, in their attempt to help, try to show how to budget finances, how to cook and keep house, how to raise children, etc. without the invitation of both the new husband and wife. This may occur when there is an inability for the husband or wife to "leave and cleave" (see Gen. 2). The specific problem is that home ties have never been cut; the mother or father talks about "my boy" and continues to try to hang on to them. Or, my "little girl," not recognizing that they are not their little girl any longer. Furthermore, problems may occur when a husband or wife demonstrates more allegiance to parents than to their mate. This can be most difficult. Another problem can occur when references are made to the way mom and dad used to do things. The way they used to do things is just that - the way they used to do things. Couples need to negotiate ways of doing things that will fit their lifestyles and belief systems.

Borrowing money from parents or children can continue to create ties which can be used manipulatively. I am not saying that it is never okay to borrow money in certain situations, because we need one another's help. I is important to be clear concerning the terms of those loans. As related previously, there can be an unwillingness to assume responsibility for the care of elderly family members. Contrary to what the world says, it is the Christian's responsibility to care for their elderly family members. Where necessary, this can include nursing homes if that is where the best care can be provided for your loved one.

Furthermore, with in-laws, there can be a difference in philosophy or life style. Opposing views between the parents and the children, such as Christian versus non-Christian, traditional versus conservative, even Republican versus Democrat, can stir trouble. Another problem can occur when parents live too close, or in the same house. It is important for young couples develop boundaries, as has been discussed earlier. They should be able to assertively state what the boundaries are to their parents so that lines of mutual respect can be developed.

Some very practical suggestions for couples to insure the establishing of good relationships with in-laws include:

- Remember the scriptural admonition that you are to leave father and mother and cleave to your spouse (Gen. 2:24, Eph. 5:21). Furthermore..
- Honor and respect your parents, but live independently of them, in separate homes if at all possible. It is important to...
- Establish priorities by putting your mate first. It is wonderful to help out mom and dad when they are in a time of need, but recognize that since you have left home and are now cleaving to your spouse, that your spouse must have number one priority in your family. Also...
- Remember that your children are your responsibility. Your parents or in-laws may have wisdom or they may not. You are responsible. Do not assume your parents or in-laws will be instantaneous baby-sitters. It is wise to establish...

- Agreed upon procedures for the treatment, discipline, etc., of your children. This can be a most difficult problem, where loving negotiation and a firm agreement by the mom and dad is essential. Do not use the kids as pawns to reward or punish the grandparents, nor should you allow your parents or in-laws to manipulate you through the children. All destructive communication should be avoided.

- Wherever possible do not borrow money from parents or depend on them economically if arrangements can be made...or at least make arrangements to pay them back.

- Don't take advantage of them because they are willing to help.

- When your parents get to a place of being unable to take care of them, be willing to provide for them. This often takes planning early in life for the special granny flat and for the finances to take care of them in their time of need.

- Keep in touch with them on a regular basis - by telephone, by visiting or by letter. Remember their special days. This is just as important to them as it is to you.

- Change your perception of your parents, recognizing that they are adults and have needs just as we do.

- Respect the counsel of parents in light of the total situation and follow their counsel when possible. Remember what Mark Twain said about his parents - it was amazing to him that when he left home at 18 how stupid his father was, and yet how bright he had become by the time Mark Twain had become age 21. Our parents have great wisdom that they can offer to us, although they do not necessarily have all the answers.

- Recognize that new relationships are developing and are part of the growth process.
- If possible live a distance away from your relatives to give opportunity for separation to occur and natural boundaries to develop.

One of the most exciting possibilities for a young couple is the ability to develop adult relationships with their parents based upon mutual respect. They tend to be very warm and satisfying, in fact, they can be of great support to both your in-laws, your own parents, and for your children as well.

STEWARDSHIP: THE THREE "T'S"

Stewardship has to do with how we manage our life under Christ's kingdom mandate. There are three primary aspects to stewardship: Time, Talent and Treasure.

Our time belongs to God, and we must be careful to manage our time judiciously. Time should follow our values...God first; spouse second, family, church, work, friends, recreation, etc. What we put first as it relates to our time speaks of our heart priorities. We must have right priorities and govern our lives accordingly to please God.

Talent has to do with our natural and spiritual gifts. We all have them, and are to dedicate them to the Lord for his service.

The third area and by far the most potentially problematic in family life has to do with treasure of money. Thus, finances will be the focus of our next discussion.

FINANCIAL PLANNING: SCRIPTURAL PRINCIPLES

A study of family life would not be complete without reviewing scriptural principles regarding finances. This section will only present a brief overview of principles and guidelines from a Christian perspective. If you have financial difficulties, or if you are just starting out on your family journey, I would strongly recommend that you find a qualified, professional, Christian, financial planner that can help you to work your way out of debt, or to help you in developing your long-term financial goals.[14]

GOD'S PLAN

Financially, we are to be good stewards. All we have belongs to God (Ps. 24:1), not merely the 10% that we hopefully give on Sunday morning. One of the best barometers of the Christian life is the way we handle our money. There are four scriptural areas that need to be considered in financial planning. The first is earning.

EARNING

In 1 Corinthians 4:7 the Word of God says that God gives us the ability to earn our money. Furthermore, Proverbs 14:25 tells us we need to work hard to earn our income. Most of us recognize that there are no free gifts. Most of us must work hard to earn the money that we have. In Proverbs 20:4 it says that the sluggard begs during harvest. They may beg, but they usually don't receive. In 2 Thessalonians Paul tells us that the man that does not

---

[14] For a comprehensive view on stewardship, both personal and within the church, an excellent training course is available titled *Resourcing Your Vision: A Comprehensive Guide to Stewardship,* by Dick Edic, from Vision Resourcing, available from Vision Publishing.

work should not eat. We are responsible to do the best that we can to earn our money, using the gifts that God has given us, while recognizing that it is God that gives us the ability to do so. Nevertheless, we need to labor hard to ensure that we have the money we need to provide for our families.

SAVINGS

Area two is savings. Proverbs 21:20 states that a wise man saves for the future. Why should we save? We should save for emergencies and prepare for retirement. Although we all hope that Jesus will return in our lifetime, no man knows the hour that the Son of Man will come and we need to be prepared for the long haul. Savings encourages us to delay or prolong our gratification for things. One of the biggest problems for most couples is plastic money - spending money before they have it – having not learned to control their spending habits. Saving money encourages us to delay our gratification for the things that we want. It provides for our children and for their future, and it teaches us self-discipline, which we all need.

SPENDING

The third area is spending. In Romans 13:8 it says that we are to owe no man anything. In our day and time, if you are going to own a home or buy a car, it is made easier to obtain them by using somebody else's money. It is a realistic goal to become debt free as soon as possible, owing only love to our fellow man. 1 Timothy 5:8 says we are to provide for our family first. It is your own family you must provide for first, not somebody else's; providing for your family is a scriptural mandate.

GIVING

The fourth area is giving. In Philippians 4:17 it says that it increases heavenly treasure (to our account) when we give. In Philippians 4:10 it tells us we can rejoice in giving and in receiving. The reasons for giving are listed in 1 Corinthians 9:7-10, 14, and 15. The Scripture states that there is joy for the giver. It is a true statement that we cannot out-give God. When we give to Him, especially when we give sacrificially, God blesses and rewards us, if we are giving with right motivation and according to the Holy Spirit's leading.

Furthermore, we often get what we pray for. If we never pray for financial resources, we are not likely to receive them. It is okay to pray for money, not so that we can use it totally for our own benefit, but so that we can use it to provide for our family, for retirement, for our children, for the church, and for the Kingdom of Heaven. God is to be thanked for our ability to give and for what we receive from Him.

Of course, it is important that we understand the basic rules for giving. They include 2 Corinthians 8:5 - we must give of ourselves first, not just our money. Romans 12:1, we must give ourselves as a living sacrifice. God desires our hearts more than He does our finances. Deuteronomy 16:17 - we are to give according to our income. 1 Corinthians 16:2 - we are to give without boasting, not making a public display as to how much you can give, but giving from your heart. Luke 6:38 - we are to give with freedom, not because we have to, but because we get to. Romans 12:8 - we are to give with simplicity. 1 Corinthians 16:2 - we are to give regularly. We should not save it all and give it all at once, but give on a regular basis. This helps us learn discipline in giving and the joy of giving on a regular basis, as an active part of our worship. I Corinthians instruct us to give cheerfully, for God loves a cheerful giver. Giving includes or generosity to the church, but should expand to those in need as God give opportunity.

Finances can cause tremendous problems for many people. Difficult situations arise in families because of their inability to handle money. Again, be encouraged to ask for help if you need it. A simple way to find out where you stand in regards to your money situation would be to develop a list of assets and liabilities, current bills and debts, matched to your income and spending habits. Ministries such as Crown Financial can help you in this regard, and you are recommended to them. This information will provide a picture of ones current financial condition and would be a first step to insuring that you are operating according to sound financial procedures.

GAINING THE PROPER PERSPECTIVE ON FINANCES

Financial problems account for much of the family discord seen in counseling offices. Almost half of all the couples going for counseling report severe money problems, yet very few are in difficulty because of inadequate cash flow or funds. We have found in many counseling situations that mates misuse money to get even with each other. Adults buy expensive things to reassure themselves that they are important. Husbands especially, who are unsure of their masculinity, are threatened if they let their wives handle the family finances. Most Christians are willing and able to practice self-control in many areas of their lives, yet have little restraint when it comes to money. The point being made in simple terms is, is money your master?

Let's look at Luke 16:10-13. Here is a picture of Christ's attitude towards money. In Jesus' opinion, it appears as though money was a little thing, somewhat inconsequential to Him. Yet, even in little things Jesus wanted faithfulness as an indicator of our heart. If we can be faithful in little things, we can be faithful in much to Him. It is important to remember, however, that money is not what true riches are, they are to be used wisely and faithfully for the Kingdom of God and to meet the basic needs we have here on earth. It is impossible for us to serve God and money at the same time; we will be a slave to one or the other. It is vital that we keep this in proper perspective.

How do Christians become a slave to money? The question really is, whom do you love, money or Christ? What is your heart attitude? If 10% of your money is dedicated to God, we are a slave to money. 1 Corinthians 10:31, it says that God expects 100% dedication. The 10% is but a mere token which says, "All I have belongs to God." In Matthew 25:14-30 it indicates that giving should be in proportion to what we receive, the more we receive, the more we should give. But, remember that 100% of who we are and what we have belongs to God, for He is the one that has given us the ability to earn it in the first place.

CATEGORIES FOR EXPENDITURES

Categories for expenditures are another area that should be clearly delineated, which should include support for the l church at home and abroad. The major categories, which should be planned for include:

- Living expenses which include food, shelter, clothing, taxes, medical expenses, transportation, repairs, and insurance. Also...

- Life improvement categories such as vacation, books, hobbies, recreation.
- Economic security is a major concern and includes life insurance, bank accounts, savings, and investments. In financial planning, a couple must consider any and all of these categories and plan or budget accordingly, with proper priorities. Certainly we must take care of the...
- Basic needs of the family and be certain to honor the Lord with your tithes and offerings. Then, you need to...
- Plan towards the future.

As you submit yourself to the Holy Spirit and wise counsel, you can be financially secure in time, with good stewardship.

SHOPPING WISDOM

Another area of consideration is how to make sense with our dollars, especially when we shop. When we shop, if at all possible, buy with cash. The most serious money problems come over the misusing of credit cards and overspending our means. As Westerners, we must learn to save for the "niceties" of life. Furthermore, make the merchant work for your money. Be careful of deals, ask questions, shop around for the best prices. Know your market - read food and other ads to know what a good price is and what is not. Develop a sense of sales resistance. There is an old saying that says, "I can resist anything, but temptation." Many of us are that way when a salesman comes and makes a good presentation. We must learn to resist and only buy those things that are needful for the family. Ask for God's wisdom (Proverbs 3:5-6) which says, "Trust in the Lord with all your heart and lean not on your own understanding. In all your ways acknowledge Him, and He will direct your path." As we trust in the Lord, He will direct us in the way that we should go and how we should wisely spend our money.

FINAL THOUGHTS ON FINANCE

Over the past few years there has been a significant amount of teaching attempting to link our spirituality with our material wealth. Certainly, God wants to prosper His people so that we have something to give. Our Lord is more interested in character than charisma and much more interested in faithfulness than financial abundance. Paul the apostle's perspective found in I Timothy 6:6-11, provides a sobering balance. God's desire is not for us to be poor. If wealth comes our way, I hope we can be good stewards for the Kingdom of God.

> *"But godliness actually is a means of great gain, when accompanied with contentment. For we have brought nothing into the world, so we can not take anything out of it either. And if we have food and covering, with these we shall be content. But those who want to get rich fall into temptation and a snare and many foolish and harmful desires which plunge men into ruin and destruction. For the love of money is a root of all sorts of evil and some by longing for it have wondered away from the faith and pierced themselves with many a pang."* (I Timothy 6:6-10)

HARMONY WITHIN THE FAMILY

As this section concludes our focus returns to the family as a whole. In spite of the many pressures that families face and the many tasks that need to be learned, God is truly for the family. As the families creator, He is most invested in it's success. Success in family life can be best summarized as having peace or harmony in the home.

A CENTRAL TRUTH

Harmony in the home is the result of all the members of the family accepting their God-given roles and working together with grace and mercy.

In Dr. Ken Chant's marvelous work "The Christian Life"[15] he provides a clear understanding as to the characteristics of a harmonious Christian Life. Two of these characteristics which must be applied in the home environment is *"epekeis"* or sweet reasonableness and love.

JUST BE REASONABLE

Sweet reasonableness encourages several issues of heart and behavior. They include: Putting away the negative, fault finding, anger and criticalness and putting on a tender heart of forgiveness. (Eph. 4:31-32). It also includes the putting on of passionate mercy, kindness, meekness, patience and humility, while putting off quarreling over petty things that a day from now will not matter (Col. 3:12-13).

Learning to see our family members as equal, or even better children of God than we are, while supporting the

---

[15] In keeping with our previous section, love and respect would go together here.

younger with patience, never taking revenge, no matter how temporarily good it might feel is key (I Thess. 5:12). As we strive, wherever we are in our family, to be as sweet and reasonable (fair, just, logical, truthful), as we can, we set in motion the laws of reciprocity (sowing and reaping) while creating an atmosphere of peace.

ABOVE ALL ELSE

However, I have counseled many families that were essentially models of "sweet reasonableness", never a crass word was spoken, politeness was flawless, and peace was always evident. The peace of a manikin! These families had peace but at too high a cost. Somewhere along life's path they lost the fervor of love that is the life blood of true relationship. Though functional and conflict free, they were virtually dead, in need of resuscitation.

Above all else, we need to learn and walk in love towards one another. This should go without saying (and often does) in the Christian home, yet the demonstration of true love, as presented by the Apostle Paul in *I Cor. 13:4-13 is,*

> *"Love is patient, love is kind. It does not envy, it does not boast, it is not proud. It is not rude, it is not self-seeking, it is not easily angered, it keeps no record of wrongs. Love does not delight in evil but rejoices with the truth. It always protects, always trusts, always hopes, always perseveres. Love never fails. But where there are prophecies, they will cease; where there are tongues, they will be stilled; where there is knowledge, it will pass away. For we know in part and we prophesy in part, but when perfection comes, the imperfect disappears. When I was a child, I talked like a*

child, I thought like a child, I reasoned like a child. When I became a man, I put childish ways behind me. Now we see but a poor reflection as in a mirror; then we shall see face to face. Now I know in part; then I shall know fully, even as I am fully known.

And now these three remain: faith, hope and love. But the greatest of these is love.

True love, love in a family, is rarely if ever a perfect love. Only God's love is. Yet our determination as members of our families and God's family is to have love for God, our neighbor and ourselves and to demonstrate it, starting at home!

Stan E. DeKoven Ph.D.

SECTION IV

COUNSELING THE TROUBLED FAMILY

A PASTORAL PERSPECTIVE

*"Man is forever striving to solve the problems of the
world whose greatest problem he is."*
Unknown Source

Stan E. DeKoven Ph.D.

SECTION IV

INTRODUCTION

This summary will provide for some parameters presented to be used in counseling troubled families. The perspective of this section is neither self-help (though I trust it will be helpful) nor is it strictly clinical. The purpose is to provide basic assistance for spiritual leaders serving in Home Fellowships, Sunday Schools, or pastoral care ministry. Provided here is a foundation to build specialized knowledge upon and to provide a starting point for assisting families. In the Bibliography is listed several excellent references for further training in this specialized area of ministry.

THE RIGHT HEART

The most important tool any counselor has at his/her disposal is him/ herself. Hopefully, if you are involved in ministry or any other helping profession, you have a heart for assisting hurting people and have to resolve the conflicts that have inevitably emerged from the family of origin. If not, or if you assume you came from the world's only perfect family, you should reconsider this area of ministry.

It takes a compassionate heart with an understanding of the human struggle to be effective in family counseling. Identification with the infirmities or weaknesses of humanity and humility towards mankind, was/is one of the shinning characteristics of Jesus Christ. The Apostle Paul reminds us in *Phil. 2:5-11,*

"Your attitude should be the same of that of Jesus Christ: Who, being in very nature God, did not consider equality with God something to be grasped, but made himself nothing, taking the very nature of a servant, being in human likeness. And being found in appearance as a man, he humbled himself and became obedient to death— even death on a cross! Therefore God exalted him to the highest place and gave him the name that is above every name, that at the name of Jesus every knee should bow, in heaven and on earth and under the earth, and every tongue confess that Jesus Christ is Lord, to the glory of the Father."

Furthermore, in Hebrews 2:17-18, we read of our great High Priest who is touched with our infirmities and intercedes for us. It reads,

"For this reason he had to be made like his brothers in every way, in order that he might become a merciful and faithful high priest in service to God, and that he might make atonement for the sins of the people. Because he himself suffered when he was tempted, he is able to help those who are being tempted."

Finally, in Hebrews 4:14-16,

"Therefore, since we have a great high priest who has gone through the heaven, Jesus the Son of God, let us hold firmly to the faith we profess. For we do not have a high priest who is unable to sympathize with our weaknesses, but we have one who has been tempted in every way, just as we

238

*are—yet without sin. Let us then approach the
throne of grace with confidence, so that we may
receive mercy and find grace to help in our time of
need."*

Let me emphasis verse 16, since it is most important as we
consider the counseling process. Psychology has been
accurately called the secular priesthood. In the counseling
office people come to a man or woman who has
(theoretically) received special training (education), has
been ordained (licensed), and has been commissioned (in
practice) to sit in judgment over the vicissitudes of life.
They hear confession, give penance, and provide
absolution, while hopefully giving positive, new direction
for future action. The field of psychology has done some
wondrous good for many, both Christian and non-
Christian. The heart intent of all practicing therapists
(from root word Therapudee, see James 5:15) is to help
people, individuals and families, to grow, change, and be
healed.

Of course, the practice of psychology has, in many ways,
taken the place belonging to the church and the priesthood
of believers. The historical church (Protestant primarily)
abandoned their God ordained call to the healing ministry,
and only since World War II have they begun to re-take
this lost ground.

In Pastoral care, and especially in counseling marriages
and families, there is by necessity a re-establishment of the
priestly role as in few other ministry services. As ministers
in counseling, we establish, in the counseling office or other
suitable confidential setting, an opportunity to come near
to the throne of grace. In Christian counseling, a forum

whereby God ministers to the wounded is established. Those seeking counsel are generally hopeful and fearful, optimistic and pessimistic, and place what little faith they may have in your priestly ministry. They trust that God will use you as an instrument of grace, to apply knowledge, understanding, and wisdom to their life situation, so they can receive mercy and find grace in their time of need. It really is a sacred ministry which must not be taken lightly. Yet, we must also recognize that you did not, as counselor, build the house (family) that will sit before you. Neither will you have the power to change their house easily. The change will only come after an honest assessment of the house has been made, necessary repairs ordered, foundations restored (teaching) and new changes made. The power for such change, secular psychology would say, lies within the individual and through the dynamic interaction and skilled interventions of the therapist. This is a limited truth, but there is power in the process. However, true lasting change, and change in the direction of godliness, will come through the application of Biblical truths adapted to individual/family needs. Ultimately, these scriptures (among many) summarize this principle,

> *"Except the Lord build the house, they labor in vain who build it, unless the Lord guards the city, the watchman keeps watch in vain."* (Ps. 127:1) *and "Not by might, nor by power, but by my Spirit, says the Lord of hosts."* (Zech. 4:6b), *and "Do not fear or be dismayed because of this great multitude* (It feels like a multitude sometimes with families) *for the battle is not your but God's."* (II Chron. 20:15b).

As a couple or family enters the sanctuary established for God to minister in, you will apply the best of your knowledge and technique. At times the dynamics of the family system, the immaturity and selfishness of the people, and the stubbornness or resistance to change may seem overwhelming (it is to all counselors), thus it is important to remember. The families ministered to do not belong to the counselor, but to the Lord, and with God's help a good counselor will be a skilled helper for them.

FAITH WORKING THROUGH LOVE:

THREE STAGES OF FAMILY COUNSELING

(CHRISTIAN COUNSELING TODAY OCT. 1992)

In an issue (Oct 1992) of the Journal for the American Association for Christian Counselors, a brief summary of family counseling was proposed.

Family counseling techniques that work are based on the biblical principle of "faith working through love" (Gal. 5:6). That principle is systematically inserted into each of these three stages of counseling.

INITIAL STAGE

Tasks: Form a good relationship with the family and assess the family's problems.

How faith working through love 8 is used:

- Demonstrate how you value each person as the basis for a good counseling relationship.

- Observe instances of a family member's failure to value each other or their active devaluing of one another.
- Suggest that a failure in love may be the main underlying cause of the problems.
- Carefully assess the major areas where this failure to love is manifested in the family.
- Solicit agreement or an understanding of the problem from family the members.
- Emphasize that change will require hard work.
- Stress the necessity of faith in Jesus Christ and encourage the family members to have faith that works by love, which will work over time.

INITIAL STAGE EXPANDED

The building of a therapeutic (caring, empathetic, nurturing) relationship takes both heart and head, art and science. For some counselors with more accepting and nurturing personas, this is quite easy and natural. For others, it must be developed through conscious effort and practice. To demonstrate faith working through love, the following combination of heart and head is needed.

DEMONSTRATING VALUE

To value someone is to prize them or esteem them as a person of worth in their own right, regardless of present circumstance. Most people in counseling, and especially couples and families will feel a sense of failure in their life walk or they would not be in your office.

One way to establish a positive basis for exploration that will lead to change is to express empathy, warmth and respect to each member for the family. This is accomplished by what you do and say, and especially by when and how you do and say affirming, caring words to each member in counseling.

For example, I will usually begin each counseling time with a social phase, where I will, in a friendly but in not too exuberant a manner greet each person individually, and introduce myself to them(if our first visit). As I do so, I make sure, if possible, to smile, offer my hand, and make good but level eye contact if possible (this can be difficult and ill advised in some cultures).

Empathy is expressed best in a non-verbal focus of the counselors' attention on the clients dilemma. Whether you agree with the clients' perspective or their problem is secondary to caring about them and trying to understand their pain. Leading statements like; "Tell me more", "I'm listening", "That must really hurt," etc... can help transmit to the client that you truly care. Simple eye contact, nodding of the head, leaning forward towards the client, or even moving your chair close to one member or the other of the family (joining) can be a measured way of showing empathy. General kindness and attentive interest that is genuine will help to exude the care needed to establish a therapeutic environment.

Warmth is expressed in several ways, and can include a firm hand shake, a smile, a positive comment for the individuals or families courage to seek help, and assurance that together answers and change is possible. Also, the office you counsel in can establish an environment conducive to counseling. A warm atmosphere with clean furniture, warm colors, even soft music is positive.

Value is expressed when you show respect for all members
of the family. We show respect through our affirming the
decision to get help while honoring the efforts they have
made thus far to solve their problems. Obviously, they have
made some positive actions or the marriage/family would
not be intact. Affirming the decisions made helps to
establish some self aspect which can go a long way towards
helpful and therapeutic decisions to change.

OBSERVATION

One of the primary and essential skills of a counselor is the
power of observation. The behaviors exhibited by
individuals and families, which include their thoughts and
verbalizations, can be most complex. Understanding the
subtle and not so subtle behaviors and attitudes of the
family provide the matrix of our diagnoses. Observation
skills, which will increase with time and experience, are
key to therapeutic intervention.

WHAT TO OBSERVE

Essentially, the counselor begins his/her observation of the
client from the first contact. In most cases (unless they
"drop in" on pastor) the first contact is by phone. As such, it
is important to remember that the person making the call
is usually the one in greatest distress. A spouse may call
for help because of their husband, wife or child, but
ultimately the caller is experiencing the most pain. The
next primary contact is the first visit. If you have a waiting
or reception room and the luxury of a secretary, having a
questionnaire, etc... is usually a good touch. Either you or
your secretary should passively observe how the family
interacts in the reception area, who does the paper work,
level of tension, where they sit in relationship to one

another, etc... Much can be learned regarding how the family reacts in tandem, but judgments should be withheld since you are just beginning your observation and your waiting room and office are artificial environments.

Once the paperwork is completed you invite the family into your office, where enough space for everyone to sit should be provided. I find having a loveseat or sofa and individual chairs in a semi-circle of sorts is best, and the counselor should not sit behind a desk. After introducing yourself to each family member, observe where and how the members sit together (or apart). You will want to have a social phase of counseling, some simple chit chat that is appropriate (such as "did you have a hard time finding the office?"). The make a comment (positive) about the family, etc. Also, take time to review and make comments/ask questions from the paperwork completed. Write what has been answered, what has not, what areas are uncomfortable, etc... Depending on your comfort with increased tension, you might use some quite reflection on your part to increase tension. It is normal for the clients' to be thinking "What is the counselor thinking of us? Can he help? Is he/she good, bad?. Remember, observation goes both ways. Hopefully, your observations will be less clouded by perceptual distortions.

From the first session on, you should write down, without analysis, your observations and ask yourself the hard questions that need answers in order for you to provide help to the clients.

Observations continue as you listen to the unique story of the family. Each member of the family including children, have a perception that carries a picture of the home. This includes the history of the strengths and weaknesses, hopes, dreams and disappointments of the family. The counselor becomes a mirror of reflection for the family, with the hope of clarifying perceptual deceptions (truth search) and providing a more merciful judgment on past and future. You will do so through your clarifying statements, probing (not intrusive) questioning, biblical principle application, and reframing of comments and behaviors to give richer meaning. You may also gather information through the plethora of testing tools available to the counselor.

There are10 key factors in assessing a family. The following help to integrated relevant elements from various models into a framework for assessing families. It is formulated in A's.[16]

- Attributes- What specials features, distinguishing strengths, remarkable traits of the family are observed?
- Abilities- What problem solving skills, coping abilities and competencies does the family possess and practice (or not)?
- Affection- How or is intimacy, caring express in ways to satisfy needs?
- Affiliation- What level of belonging, do family members experience; how are boundaries established and expressed; are there splits or alliances in the family that need to be addressed?
- Autonomy- Is there differentiation, dependency issues, stability or instability, and developmental concerns with the family?

---

[16] Adapted From Raymond Fox, Elements of the Helping Process, Hawrath Presss, New York, 2001, pgs 193-194

- Arrangement of the family infrastructure- Do triangles in communication, spousal or sibling subsystems, dysfunctional roles and/scapegoating occur?
- Atmosphere- Is the family warm, cool, trusting, conflictual, controlling?
- Adaptation to the environment- How has the family adapted culturally, religiously and socially?
- Artifacts- What family rules, rituals, rites of passage are important to the family, and how are they expressed or repressed?
- Anomalies- What myths, secretes and areas of uniqueness is seen in the family?

Another helpful tool for counselor to use in understanding the dynamics of the family is a Genogram. The genogram looks at the multi-generational aspects of family problems. Information is collected and illustrated (see figure __) which helps both the counselor and the family see how problems may have been inherited from previous generations. Once discovered (an enlightening process in itself), prayer can be a powerful tool in helping the family (see the author's *I Want To Be Like You, Dad* for more on this topic).

Once you have gathered data on your clients, usually after 2-3 sessions, taking detailed notes, or cassette recording of your observations, you will want to summarize your information into a usable format. There are many systems available, many which can be found in the author's book *The Healing Community: How to Start a Counseling Ministry*. Once you begin using this system you will develop your own short hand modification which will work best for you.

First, it is helpful to provide identifying information at the top of your form or report. Included will be names, addresses, phones, employer, ages, etc... Secondly, you will want to detail the presenting problem, preferably in the words or with the perceptions of each member of the family. Direct quotes are helpful. Since this is a summary, you want to keep this to a maximum of 1 written page. Thirdly, a history of the family, provided through your life history questionnaire, self-report (asking questions during counseling on where they met, what they like best about each other, early problems, late problems) or perhaps a genogram should be written to get a clear picture of how the symptoms/complaints of the clients relate to the family of origin. Remember, many of the symptoms can be traced 3-4 generations, where some specialized ministry may be needed. Fourth, you will record, in outline form, your observations of the clients, without analyzing. Fifth, after some time of reflection and prayer, you will make conclusions or diagnosis of the family. This conclusion is a series of statements about the client which reviews the history, symptoms, observations, etc., which describes the why the client is where they are and on the how they came to the condition they are in. Finally, you will want to make a plan for assisting the family.

Again, you will be making some concrete statements to bring change to the family. These statements or interventions should be made in collusion with the family. Only what they commit to do will actually come to pass. Goals should be made with specific strategies that relate to the problems stated, as well as to strengthen the fundamental foundations of the family. Areas to cover may include:

- Skill building or communication, priority setting, self-control, or self-gratification modification, etc...
- Relationship enhancement through spending quality time, building a basis for forgiveness, learning to love, connecting with the larger Christian community.
- Conflict resolution through time-out/fair fighting tactics.
- Individual development through personal or group study, prayer together as a couple, etc.
- Life changes/decisions that must be made to ensure the continuation of the relationship.

When completed, this report becomes the working document for counseling purposes. Your goals for counseling with the family are to be written to activate the family to be active participants of their growth and change (if they truly want to change) over the next phase of counseling.

CONCLUSION TO THE INITIAL PHASE

As with medicine, a poor, incomplete or false diagnosis can lead to disastrous results. Fortunately with families, and due to the reality that counseling is an inexact science, there is room for trying different techniques and making preliminary conclusions that more data, uncovered at a later date, may mildly or significantly modify. Finally, you must know when you are over your head. There are families that are, as it were ,"professional patients." You are probably not their first counselor nor will you be their last. They have more interest in the "game" than change. Use wisdom and know your limitations, including when to refer.

MIDDLE STAGE

Tasks: The goal of this stage is to break up old patterns of family behavior and build new patterns, which is the hard work of ministry to troubled families.

How faith working through love is used:

- Examine specific family interactions that are problems, showing how problems are related to failures in love (and repeat).
- Help families devise new patterns of behavior that show love.
- Help family members practice those patterns within the counseling session.
- Help family members plan ways to show love and encourage them to practice these behaviors at home.

MIDDLE STAGE EXPANDED

As stated in the above outline, the primary task of the middle stage (sessions 3-20 or so) is to "break up old patterns." Thus, once the primary negative patterns are identified you will utilize family strengths supplemented with well chosen interventions to work through the problems you may choose to focus on one at a time or several at once. I usually attempt to steer the family towards resolving ones with a high degree of generalization to their patterns first. However, I will yield to the wisdom of the family if they are insistent. An example may suffice.

THE SMITH FAMILY

The Smith family, George, Ciela, Jane and James were referred for George's behavior which resulted in economic uncertainty, severe family tension, resentment over unfulfilled promised needs, and general family depression. Several problems came to the forefront, including:

- James rebellion.
- George's anger, which cost him jobs, the family relationships, feeling out of control.
- Ciela's controlling of George and the rest of the family (caretaking).
- Jane's (age 11) clinging, demanding behavior towards mom, extreme dependency.

The family wanted George to just stop being angry (he had been raised in an alcoholic home with much domestic violence), assuming that that would "solve the problem." My role was to "fix" dad. The family wanted (to include George) to provide tools (magic) to change George's behavior. However, I saw the family in a collusive dance to keep the family from growing past the adolescence of dad or the mother role of mom, which the parents were fixed in. The son and daughter needed significant help in making this transformation.

My first interview was used to make a minor role adjustment between father and son, requiring a change in the whole family. I instructed the father and son (who had a mutually antagonistic relationship) to work on a project together that would require time, mutual respect and support, and would be fun when completed. My assumption was that this "project" (building a remote control boat.

Something they both had wanted to do) would be very difficult. The difficulty would come from various fronts (sabotage from growth always comes), especially from Ciela. Thus, the rules were that only father and son could participate, and mom could not help in any way, and the father and son team would work together every Saturday until finished. The purpose was to break up the push-pull relationship over control of the children, create opportunity for George and James to bond and succeed, and created opportunity for mom to focus on Jane, which made her (Jane) symptoms progressively (temporarily) worse.

Over several weeks, I was able to use this phenomenon to bring to the forefront mom's need to be the caretaker. I was able to assist her in letting go of her mothering behavior. Eventually we worked on the lack of fulfillment and intimacy in the marital relationship. Thus, from one small intervention, many mini-changes can and will occur.

You can best assist the family in breaking old patterns by crowding them out with new, healthier ones. Rather than setting your sights on "digging out" all of the old self-destructive patterns, your quest is to minister truth that will be received and acted upon. Some "putting off the old" (Eph. 4:22) is likely to occur and is certainly required, but it is ill advised to set the resolution of deeply held unconscious conflicts as a realistic goal. That is best handled by the Holy Spirit and advanced clinical training.

PRACTICE, PRACTICE, PRACTICE

During this middle stage is where the majority of family counseling techniques are used. Though I will mention and illustrate some, it is beyond the scope of this book to present technically oriented interventions. However, all techniques have at their core the purpose of creating greater awareness within the family as to blockages in family growth, as well as to provide opportunity to act out new, potentially healing behaviors that will hopefully establish new life style patterning. Thus, as various techniques are used, the goal is to make the family aware and provide ample opportunity (usually during the week between counseling sessions) to practice, practice, practice.

One technique used fairly universally by family counselors is called Describing the Symptom. In this technique the counselor simply and authoritatively makes the seemingly obvious, obvious. That is, patterns, hidden agendas, family of origin patterns (Grandad was an alcoholic, Dad is an alcoholic, son is using drugs and drinking) etc., which are evident to the counselor but not fully evident to the family are brought into the open. Again, this will bring awareness if properly timed. You then give "permission" for members of the family to track similar patterns or spy (usually one of the children is already doing this and thus becomes an ally) out the family and report in the next session. Hopefully, over time the family learns to catch themselves before acting according to past behaviors.

Family sculpting or shaping, popularized by Prof. Virginia Satir, M.S.W., takes family members and molds them in ways to over exaggerate or exacerbate family symptoms. For example: if the father is perceived as a mean, ominous bear, "sculpting him" by putting him on a chair, arms raised, teeth bared and growling with the family cowering in fear, can create awareness of the father's effect. This awareness then leads to ways father can behave when feeling bearish, instead of growling.

Furthermore, new behaviors can be taught to the family to assist them in responding to the bear besides growling, (time-out, confrontational). In other cases, role-reversal, another similar technique, places mother and/or family on a chair and dad in the weaker role (usually disdainful and resisted by all) to create awareness. Depending on the process that develops, empathy for the bear cub that is the child inside the father can develop themes of punishment and revenge can be explored, helping father deal with fears of weakness, etc. may emerge.

Another variation of family sculpting or role-reversal is the use of an empty chair. While sitting in the chair (a technique first developed by Fritz Perls, who would probably not approve of my usage) the family has the opportunity to affirm the chosen one without negative intent. This affirmation can be most powerful. The hope is to "call forth" the positive as well as to bring to awareness some of the good and reinforcing it. Harping on the negative is not allowed and generally should be discouraged completely. Similar to the empty chair is a joining or bonding technique (counselor to family member) called overexageration of the symptom. This can be used in the positive (as in the empty chair) or negative. As an example, a client (husband) is describing his wife as a stupid woman and lousy housekeeper and the counselor "joins" with his statement, extending it to "THE worst of all time housekeeper, slob, filth bag, ignoramus, etc..." Your hope is to create an initial sense of identification and then guilt or even gallantry on the husbands' part. Even a "Well, she's not that bad!" would give you, the counselor, opportunity to bring balance. This technique, however, should be used with caution.

Finally, the most commonly used techniques to assist the family in skill building is accomplished through positive, "truth in love" communication. These exercises, of which there are hundreds, are used to build bridges, open up lines of intimacy and create new avenues for relationship enhancement. Family meetings, holding hands while talking, teaching "I" messages, giving feed back, trust exercises, sensate focus, are but a few of the techniques.

CONCLUSION TO THE MIDDLE STAGE

Ultimately, the hard work of counseling occurs during this phase. Working things through to perfection is unreasonable. Positive adjustment, small but significant changes are hopeful and to be worked toward until the family can begin to show love and respect in action in the home. In other words, when they develop a more consistent pattern of healthy days than unhealthy, you are moving towards the end of this stage. As a rule of thumb, for four weeks of positive change or maintained growth without major regression is s a guide to entering the last stage.

ENDING STAGE

Tasks: The task is to consolidate changes and end formal counseling.[17]

How faith working through love is used:

- Review changes that have been tried throughout counseling and help the family members evaluate the effectiveness of the changes.

---

[17] The hope is that the family has been properly integrated into a strong and supportive faith community for continued care and accountability.

- Express confidence in the family's ability to sustain changes with continued practice of new ways of relating.

ENDING STAGE EXPANDED

All endings are a rehearsal for our own death, or the death of a loved one. At least I heard someone say that once. I am not fully convinced that ALL are, but certainly there is some truth to the statement. Saying good-bye is not easy.

For pastors, if you are counseling a parishioner, hopefully you will not be saying good-bye but simply transitioning back as "just" members of the congregation. Hopefully, they have remained active participants or become more active through the counseling process (a part of my normal agreement to counsel!). However, since counseling is a very special relationship, some working through the good-bye is needed.

To begin with, I recommend that there always be a "summary" session, where you review the change and new covenant or commitments that have been made in the process. This is usually like looking at old home movies, with times of tears and laughter.

Secondly, the counselor is able to give final instructions and express confidence in the families ability to sustain and even make new changes. Furthermore, they can be assured that you can and will be a continued resource to them if significant issues arise that the family cannot solve without the counselor. Most clients will state that they incorporate the "therapist/ counselor" into their heads, and they will consciously or unconsciously ask the question "what/how the counselor would handle it, etc..." This "voice" will ultimately fade and simply become a part of the family wisdom. For safety sake, I will usually schedule a 3 mo., 6 mo. or 1 year (depending on the family) or all three "check up" on the family. This provides a sense of outside accountability and a safety valve. The family can take or leave the appointment as needed.

CONCLUSION TO THE CONCLUSION

In ministry to families, prevention is always best. However, when counseling is required, doing it within the context of the local church is highly recommended. The support network found in a loving congregation, and the accountability found through relationships in the Body of Christ can strengthen the treatment process. These brief suggestions should get you started in the counseling process, and hopefully wet your appetite for furthermore study.

HELPS IN FAMILY COUNSELING

"God is our refuge and strength, a very present help in trouble."
Ps 46:1

A MODEL FOR RESOLVING FAMILY CONFLICT

- Recognize conflict issues - don't ignore them.
- Listen carefully to the other person. Proverbs 18:13
- Select an appropriate time.
- Specifically define the conflict.
  a. How do you define the conflict?
  b. How do you think the other person defines the conflict?
  c. What behaviors contribute to the conflict, in your opinion?
  d. What behaviors do you think the other person sees as contributing to the conflict?
  e. What are the issues of agreement and disagreement?
- Identify your own contribution to the problem.
  a. Choose one word which best describes what you want to discuss.
  b. State the word or subject in one complete sentence. Be precise and specific.
- Identify several alternate solutions.
- Decide on a mutually acceptable solution.
  a. What are the steps in implementation?
  b. What are the possible outcomes?
- Implement new behaviors.

PARENT-TEEN RELATIONSHIPS - WHAT DO YOU THINK?

AGREE   DISAGREE   STATEMENT

____   ____   1. An argument is a destructive force in the home between parents and teens

____   ____   2. Quarreling is wrong for a Christian family even though insights are gained thereby.

____   ____   3. The wisest course to take when an argument seems to be developing is to remain silent or leave the room.

____   ____   4. An adolescent should always obey a parent without questioning what he says or his authority.

____   ____   5. Parents should have a voice in who their son or daughter dates

____   ____   6. Teenagers will take responsibility when they are ready to do so.

____   ____   7. Most of the problems between parents And teenagers occur because the parents fail to listen to or understand the teenager.

____   ____   8. A good method of discipline with teenagers is focusing upon what they did wrong so they will not do the same thing again.

____   ____   9. It is a sign of spiritual and emotional immaturity for a Christian to be angry with another person.

____   ____   10. A teenager should be given a choice when it comes to participating in family devotions or worship. He can choose whether he wants to or not.

____   ____   11. Nagging another person is sometimes necessary in order to get him to respond.

_____ _____ 12. It is all right to modify the truth to avoid unpleasantness in the home.

_____ _____ 13. Parents make lots of mistakes. Therefore teenagers should be careful to obey them only when they are right.

_____ _____ 14. Since parents brought their teenagers into the world, they owe it to them to give them clothes, food, a place to live, and plenty of attention.

_____ _____ 15. If a teenager obeys and respects his parents, he will always cooperate and be understanding.

FAMILY EVALUATION

- If you were to describe or define your own family life with one word, what would the word be?
- What strengths do you see in your own family?
- What strengths do you see in your parents or teens? Have you ever told them that you are aware of these strengths and appreciate them?
- Write down the goals you have for your family life.
- What do you think parents or teens would say about your family?
- What do your parents or teens do that make you feel loved or of value?
- What do you do that expresses your love toward your family?
- What expectations does God have for your family?
- What do you feel is a weak area in your family life?
- What can you do to strengthen this weak area and what can you do to reach the goals that you have for your family life?

FAMILY MEETING IN SESSION

- Any "excitements," news, or "appreciations?"
- Any hopes or wishes?
- Any "puzzles" or questions?
- Complaints with your recommendations for change - what do you want? Use "I - messages."
- Any complaints?
- New information or family plans?

LISTENING TO OTHERS

1. *STOP TALKING* - you can't listen while you are talking.
2. *EMPATHIZE WITH THE OTHER PERSON* - try to put yourself in his place so that you can see what he is trying to get at.
3. *ASK QUESTIONS* - when you don't understand, when you can't follow him, when you want to show him you are listening. Don't ask questions that will embarrass him or show him up.
4. *DON'T GIVE UP TOO SOON* - Don't interrupt the other person; give him time to say what he has to say.
5. *CONCENTRATE ON WHAT HE IS SAYING* - actively focus your attention on his words, his ideas, and his attitude toward the subject.
6. *LOOK AT THE OTHER PERSON* - his face, his mouth, his eyes, his hands; all this will help him communicate with you. It helps you concentrate and makes him feel like you are listening.
7. *SMILE AND GRUNT APPROPRIATELY* - but don't overdo it.
8. *LEAVE YOUR EMOTIONS BEHIND* (if you can) - try to push your worries, your fears, your problems, outside the conference room. They may prevent you from listening effectively.

9. *CONTROL YOUR ANGER* - Try not to get angry at what he is saying; your anger may prevent you from understanding him.

10. *GET RID OF DISTRACTIONS* - put down any papers or pencils you have in your hands; they may distract your attention.

11. *GET THE MAIN POINTS* - concentrate on the main ideas and not the illustrative material; examples, stories, and statistics, are important, but usually are not the main points. Examine them only to see if they prove, support, or define the main ideas.

12. *SHARE RESPONSIBILITY FOR COMMUNICATION* - only part of the responsibility rests with the speaker; you as the listener have an important part. Try to understand, and if you don't, question him.

13. *REACT TO IDEAS, NOT TO THE PERSON* - don't let your reactions to the person influence your interpretation of what he says. His ideas may be good even if you don't like him as a person, or the way he looks.

14. *DON'T ARGUE MENTALLY* - when you are trying to understand the other person, it is a handicap to argue with him mentally as he is speaking. This sets up a barrier between you and the speaker.

15. *USE THE DIFFERENCE IN RATE* - you can listen faster than he can talk, so use this rate difference to your advantage by: trying to stay on right track, anticipate what he is going to say, think back over what he has said, evaluate his development, etc. Rate difference: speech rate is about 100 to 150 words per minute; thinking: 250 to 500.

16. *LISTEN FOR WHAT IS NOT SAID* - sometimes you can learn just as much by determining what the other person leaves out or avoids as you can by listening to what he says.

17. *LISTEN TO HOW SOMETHING IS SAID* - we frequently concentrate so hard on what is said that we miss the importance of the emotional reactions and attitudes related to what is said. His attitudes and emotional reactions may be more important than what is said in so many words.

18. *DON'T ANTAGONIZE THE SPEAKER* - you may cause the other person to conceal his ideas, emotions, attitudes by antagonizing him in any of a number of ways: arguing, criticizing, taking notes, not taking notes, asking questions, etc. Try to judge and be aware of the effect you are having on the other person. Adapt to him.

19. *LISTEN FOR HIS PERSONALITY* - one of the best ways of learning about a person is to listen to him talk; as he talks you can begin to find out what he likes and dislikes, what his motivations are, or what his value system is.

20. *AVOID JUMPING TO ASSUMPTIONS* - they can get you into trouble in trying to understand the other person. Don't assume that he uses words the same way you do; that he didn't say what he meant, but you understand what he meant; that he is avoiding looking you in the eye because he is telling a lie; that he is trying to embarrass you by looking you in the eye; that he is distorting the truth because what he says doesn't agree with what you think; that he is lying because he has interpreted the facts differently than you have; that he is unethical because he is trying to win you over to his point of view; that he is angry because he is enthusiastic in presenting his views. Assumptions like these may turn out to be true, but more often they make understanding, agreement, or compromise more difficult.

21. *AVOID CLASSIFYING THE SPEAKER* - it has some value, but beware! Too frequently we classify a person as

one type of person and then try to fit everything he says into what makes sense coming from that type of person. He is a Republican. Therefore, our perceptions of what he says or means are all shaded by whether we like or dislike Republicans. At times, it helps us to understand people to know their politics, their religious beliefs, or their jobs, but people are unpredictable and rarely fit classifications perfectly.

22. *AVOID HASTY JUDGMENTS* - wait until all the facts are in before making any judgments.

23. *RECOGNIZE YOUR OWN PREJUDICE* - try to be aware of your own feelings toward the speaker, the subject, or the occasion, and allow for these pre-judices.

24. *IDENTIFY TYPE OF REASONING* - frequently it is difficult to sort out good and faulty reasoning when you are listening. Nevertheless, it is so important that a listener should make every effort to spot faulty reasoning when he hears it.

25. *EVALUATE FACTS AND EVIDENCE* - as you listen, try to identify not only the significance of the facts and evidence, but also their relationship to the argument.

HIS NEEDS/HER NEEDS

MARITAL INTIMACY CHECK-UP

Facts of Intimacy	1) Both Desire Improvement	2) He Desires Improvement	3) She Desires Improvement	4) Both Are Satisfied

1. Sexual Intimacy ___
2. Emotional Intimacy (being tuned in to each other's wavelength) ___
3. Intellectual Intimacy (closeness in the world of ideas) ___
4. Aesthetic Intimacy (sharing beauty) ___
5. Creative Intimacy (doing things together) ___
6. Recreational Intimacy (sharing fun and play) ___
7. Work Intimacy (sharing common tasks) ___
8. Crisis Intimacy (coping with problems and pain) ___
9. Conflict Intimacy (facing differences) ___
10. Commitment Intimacy (mutuality derived from common self-investment) ___
11. Spiritual Intimacy (sharing ultimate concerns) ___
12. Communication Intimacy (source of all types of true intimacy) ___

Where both desire improvement develop an action plan to accomplish the improvement. Choose the priority.

Who Are You?	Who Am I?
What Are You Worth?	What Am I Worth?

MARRIAGE GOALS

KEY:
1. Actively progressing towards excellence.
2. Minimal commitment.
3. Avoiding the topic.

Husband asks wife question; then wife asks husband.

1. Do you believe our marriage is maturing and we are coming closer together?

        1.____ 2.____ 3.____

2. Do you feel we clearly communicate?

        1.____ 2.____ 3.____

3. Do you feel that I am sensitive to your personal needs?

        1.____ 2.____ 3.____

4. What would you like me to say or do the next time you seem to be angry with me or you are not speaking to me?

_____

5. The next time you are late in getting ready to go some place, what would you like me to say or do?

_____

6. What would you like me to say or do the next time you seem to be getting impatient with something or someone?

_____

7. What would you like me to say or do if you begin to criticize someone?

_____

8. Do you feel I need to improve in getting ready on time or getting to meetings on time?

        Yes____ No____

9. Do you feel we should go out together more often?

Yes____ No____

If yes, where?

_____

10. Do I make cutting remarks about you or criticize you in front of other people?

Yes____ No____

11. What should I do in public to encourage you?

_____

12. Do I respond to your suggestions and ideas as if I had already thought ofthem instead of thanking you and encouraging you to contribute more?

Yes____ No____

13. Do I tell you enough about what I do every day?

Yes____ No____

14. What little acts of love do I do for you?

_____

15. What most often causes you to get angry with me?

_____

16. Do I convey my admiration and respect often enough?

Yes____ No____

17. Do we "play act" a happy marriage in front of other people?

Yes____ No____

18. What do you think I Corinthians 7:3-7 means?

_____

19. Do you feel we need to see a marriage counselor?

Yes____ No____

20. What are the responsibilities of a "help-mate"?

_____

21. Do we give each other the same attention we did before we had children?

Yes_____ No_____

Comment:

_____

NEW COVENANT PRINCIPLES – SAMPLE

I. Husband to Wife:
    a. Love
    b. Sacrifice
    c. Provide and protect
    d. Share the common grace of God, dwell with her in peace as a weaker vessel
    e. Honor
    f. Be an Example and the Spiritual Leader of the Home.

II. Wife to Husband
    a. Respect or Submit to him
    b. Honor
    c. Love
    d. Be an Example of Godliness to the community and for the children

III. Parents to Children
    a. Raise up before the Lord
    b. Example of Godliness
    c. Nurture and love unconditionally
    d. Discipline with love, teach and correct

IV. Children to Parents
    a. Obey
    b. Honor

    c. Follow the Lord and submit as unto the Lord

V. Children to Each Other
    a. Support and assist each other
    b. Love and help each other as brother and sister,
       sister to sister, brother to brother in the Lord.

Scripture References Include: Col. 3:18-21, Eph. 5:22-6:4, I Peter 3:1-12, I John 4:7-8.

COVENANT AGREEMENT

HUSBAND AND WIFE

We agree and vow, with God as our helper, to love and honor, respect and nurture each other according to God's word and each others needs. This includes, but is not limited to the following:

I. Wife requests of Husband:

    a.

        1.
        2.
        3.
        4.

    b.

        1.
        2.

    c.

        1.
        2.

    d.

        1.
        2.

II. Husband requests of Wife:

    a.

        1.
        2.
        3.

    4.

  b.

    1.

    2.

  c.

    1.

    2.

  d.

    1.

    2.

We both agree to follow God's word, especially as seen in the following passages:

Eph. 5:22-6:4
Col. 3:18-21
I Peter 3:1-8
I Cor. 13

This agreement is spiritually binding and freely entered into before God, each other and our Pastor, and is to be a guide for our relationship, open to change as the Lord reveals the need and according to His perfect will.

WIFE_____   HUSBAND_____

DATE_____   DATE_____

PASTOR_____

DATE_____

GLOSSARY OF TERMS

Autonomy
Health, maturity, and responsible functioning resulting from an appropriately balanced blend of thinking, feeling and acting.

Body Language
Any signals a person sends by means of his body without using words or sounds.

Closed Family Style
Disharmonious blending together of family members' personal life-styles that conflict or a harmonious but non constructive blend of neurotic styles, which results in an unhealthy or dysfunctional dynamic equilibrium.

Closed Marital Relationship
A marital relationship based on demands for conformity, little freedom, a lack of awareness, and ineffective, often destructive communication and interaction.

Closed Person
Person who has little self-awareness of others and who is governed largely by unconscious, automatic, and repetitious inside and outside forces.

Closed Society
A society based on a structured, authoritarian, patriarchal system: one that maintains its stability and the stability of its members by means of a restrictive system of accepted beliefs, expectation, rules and values.

Communication
Specific and specialized form of interaction involving the conscious and unconscious process of giving and receiving verbal and nonverbal signals, messages, and responses.

Complementary Relationship
Relationship between two people in which each person's lifestyle fills in or supplies much of what is lacking or seems to be lacking in the other's lifestyle.

Dating
Any non marital, two person relationship.

Dynamics of Marital Interaction
Forces that create and constitute the activity between or among people in a relationship and the interplay among these forces.

Extended Family
Any grouping related by descent, marriage, or adoption that is broader than the nuclear family.

Family
Any group that operates in ways designed to foster group unity and that fulfills some or all of the functions designed to promote and protect the well-being of the group and its members.

Family Roles
Roles most basic to the family and interaction, which are the parents and children.

Functional Relationship
Relationship in which the dynamic equilibrium is based on clear, undistorted communication and on patterns of interaction that are not automatic or repetitious, but are under each person's conscious control.

Identity
Who a person is in the here and now, how he got to be who he is now, and who he may become in the future.

Insight
Personal understanding resulting from being able to put thoughts, feelings and the meaning of actions together in conceptual form.

Marital Concept
The way each partner sees (perceives) and feels about the marital relationship.

Marriage
One long-term or permanent heterosexual couple relationship sanctioned by religion and society.

Nonverbal Communication
Process of sending and receiving signals and messages by means of the body but not the voice.

Nuclear Family
Commonly consists of two married adults who are parents to one or more children (whether created by the spouses or adopted), all of whom ordinarily live together in an interrelated group.

Open Marital Relationship
Marital relationship based on respect for individuality, responsible use of freedom, interpersonal and interpersonal awareness and effective, constructive communication and interaction.

Open Society
Society that is based on a non-authoritarian system and that is flexible and tolerant enough to allow for the existence and encouragement of alternative ways of thinking, feeling, and acting.

Parenting
Process of a parent's (or other adults') caring for, protecting, socializing, and giving physical and emotional nurturing to a child.

Personality
Dynamic interaction between and among a person's biophysical and psychological components, the results of which inform and control both his characteristic and his unique thoughts, feelings, and actions.

Relationship
Outcome of moment-to-moment ongoing interaction between at least two people (their self-systems and lifestyles). This interaction involves achieving and maintaining some kind of interpersonal and interpersonal dynamic equilibrium.

Self-Concept
The ways a person sees and thinks about himself (self-image) and the ways he feels about himself (self-esteem).

Self-Fulfilling Prophecy
Beliefs a person holds that he makes come true because he believes and feels them to be true.

BIBLIOGRAPHY AND RECOMMENDED READINGS

Bohac, Joseph. Group Dynamics: For Christian Counselors. Ramona, California: Vision Publishing, 1995.

Bohac, Joseph. Human Development: A Christian Perspective. Ramona California: Vision Publishing, 1993.

Chant,Ken. *The Christian Life.* Ramona, California: Vision Publishing,

Christenson, Larry. *The Christian Family.* Bethany House Publishers, 1970

Clinebell, Harold   *The Intimate Marriage*

Crabb, Larry, *Effective Biblical Counseling.* Zondervan Publishing Company. 1977.

DeKoven, Stan. *Journey to Wholeness.* Ramona, California: Vision Publishing, 2004.

DeKoven, Stan. On Belay! An Introduction to Christian Counseling. Ramona, California: Vision Publishing, 1994.

DeKoven, Stan. *Parenting on Purpose: A Practical Guide to Christian Parenting.* Ramona, California: Vision Publishing, 1996.

DeKoven, Stan. I Want to be Like You, Dad. 2nd edition. Ramona, California: Vision Publishing, 2004.

DeKoven, Stan. *Grief Relief.* Ramona, California: Vision Publishing, 2006.

DeKoven, Stan. The Healing Community: Developing a Counseling Ministry for the Local Church. Ramona, California: Vision Publishing, 1988.

DeKoven, Stan. Crisis Counseling. Ramona, California: Vision Publishing, 2004.

DeKoven, Stan. Addiction Counseling: Theories and Strategies. Ramona, California: Vision Publishing, 2000.

DeKoven, Stan. *Family Violence: Patterns of Destruction.* Ramona, California: Vision Publishing, 1999.

Dobbins, R.D.   *Train Up a Child*

Dobson, James. *Dare to Discipline.* Bantam Books, 1982.

Erikson, Erik. *Identity: Youth and Crisis.* W.W. Norton & Company, 1994.

Hesselgrave, Donald. *Counseling Cross-Culturally.* Wipf & Stock Publishers, 2002.

Sanford, John *The Transformation of the Inner Man*

White, John *Eros Defiled.* InterVarsity Press, 1977.

Printed in the United States
99760LV00003B/382/A

9 781931 178174